THE ILLUSTRATED COMPUTER DICTIONARY and HANDBOOK

Les Cowan

ENRICH / OHAUS
SAN JOSE, CALIFORNIA 95131

Graphic Design by Kaye Graphics
Cartoon Illustrations by Corbin Hillam
Technical Illustrations by Terri Dennis & Kaye Quinn

Editorial Direction by Contemporary Ideas, Inc.
Edited by Jim Haugaard, Jana Morris & Matt Foley

Typography by KGN Graphics

Published by
ENRICH/OHAUS
2325 Paragon Drive
San Jose, CA 95131
U.S.A.

For information on rights and distribution outside the U.S.A., please write
ENRICH/OHAUS at the above address.

ISBN: 0-86582-116-X
Catalog No.: EN79101

Printed in the United States of America

10   9   8   7   6   5   4   3   2   1

ABOUT THE AUTHOR

Les Cowan is a native of the San Francisco Bay Area. He received his education in Journalism at the University of California, Berkeley. For the past several years he has followed an interest in video and computers, leading him to specialize in technical subjects. He has written technical material for a number of Silicon Valley companies including Hewlett-Packard and American Microsystems Inc. and he has programmed computers professionally.

He is a contributing editor to Air-Cal magazine, for whom he writes a monthly column on developments in electronics. He also contributes to a number of publications in the field, including PC World, PC Magazine, Popular Computing and InfoWorld.

ACKNOWLEDGEMENTS

The publisher wishes to acknowledge the following companies for their generosity in furnishing us with photographs for use throughout this book.

AMDAHL CORPORATION - *88*

AMDEK CORPORATION - *37, 50, 93, 108, 109, 181*

APPLE COMPUTER, INC. - *31, 36, 178, 182, 213*

ATARI INC. - *36, 49, 64, 68, 179, 215*

COMMODORE COMPUTER SYSTEMS DIVISION - *30, 80, 175, 221*

CROMEMCO INCORPORATED - *36, 93*

FORD MOTOR COMPANY - *72, 118*

GENIE COMPUTER CORPORATION - *48*

HAYES MICROCOMPUTER PRODUCTS, INC. - *95*

IBM - *89, 219*

INTEL CORPORATION - *25, 26, 32, 74, 110, 152*

MEMOREX CORPORATION - *49, 176*

NEC HOME ELECTRONICS (U.S.A.) INC. - *107, 177*

NOVATION, INC. - *77*

RADIO SHACK, A DIVISION OF TANDY CORP. - *12, 43, 51, 66, 71, 95, 102, 110, 111, 130, 137, 149, 180, 217*

TEXAS INSTRUMENTS INCORPORATED - *47, 60, 81, 96, 126, 128, 138, 159, 223*

TG PRODUCTS - *78, 104, 140*

3G COMPANY, INC. - *82, 97*

TABLE OF CONTENTS

INTRODUCTION

In the past few years a new tool, called a microcomputer, has appeared. We hear an awful lot about computer literacy, the electronic revolution, and the power of high technology to change the way we do almost everything. It is enough to either propel one onto the computer bandwagon or scare one as far as possible away from it. In fact, computers are neither mysterious puzzles, evil threats nor magic devices that will solve all our problems, or even make us happier.

What computers are, are new, unknown. But not as unknown as most people think. For example, virtually every household in the United States contains at least one remote terminal through which is accessed one of the world's largest and most powerful computer systems. Almost every one of us uses such a terminal every day. That terminal is the ordinary telephone.

The aim of this book is to present the simple facts about computers. It was written for the person who knows little or nothing about computers, but wants to learn: the computer beginner who has just bought his first computer, is preparing to buy one or is wondering if he should buy one. Its purpose is to overcome the atmosphere of complexity and confusion that has been created by marketing hype, publicity and the proliferation of confusing jargon that besets the world of computers.

The most difficult part of learning about computers is the technical terms. Even very simple concepts are rendered incomprehensible if they are presented in complicated jargon. The first part of this book is an illustrated dictionary of computer terms. It contains all the words which most often confuse a beginner. This central body of terms covers everything that the novice needs to know, plus a great many more sophisticated concepts of computer science. All definitions are written in plain, easy to understand English. Wherever possible, definitions are supported by examples and analogies to familiar concepts. Once these terms are understood and become familiar, it will be much easier to learn the underlying principles of computer design, operation and programming.

To further enhance this learning process, the dictionary has been illustrated. Many studies have conclusively demonstrated that information is easier to learn if it is presented in more than one way. If a term is accompanied by an apt picture, the student will associate picture and definition in his memory, thereby reinforcing his ability to remember what the term means.

The second part of this book is a computer handbook. Like the dictionary, it contains information about all kinds of computers, but it is biased in favor of the microcomputer user. It introduces you to the way that all computers work, discusses the history of computers, describes how programming languages are used to control computers, introduces you to the BASIC language, gives a brief summary of programming techniques, and surveys the keyboards of six popular home computers.

These are the points of interest to computer newcomers. The computer user may run a program or play a game on his computer without any computer knowledge at all. But most users want to go beyond the RUN command. Some want to know *how* the computer runs a program. Others are curious about writing a program of their own. Still others would like to know more about the way that computers evolved from simple counting devices into the powerful machines available today. Some readers will be prospective computer users, eager for help in evaluating available machines and accessories. For all these readers, *THE ILLUSTRATED COMPUTER DICTIONARY and HANDBOOK* will be an invaluable tool and aid.

The Illustrated
Computer
DICTIONARY

abacus (AB•uh•kus) *n.* A device made of beads strung on wires. Each bead stands for a number. By moving the beads, you can add, subtract, multiply and divide numbers almost as easily as by using a calculator. Abacuses are the earliest machines used for calculating. They were used in China, Egypt and Greece more than 2500 years ago.

abort (uh•BORT) *v.* Anytime you stop a computer in the middle of what it is doing, you abort it.

absolute address (AB•suh•loot AD•res) *n.* A computer's memory is divided into thousands of locations, called memory addresses. A program or other block of data may be placed in that memory starting at a certain address. A single piece of data will have an address within the block, for example, thirty addresses from the beginning of the block. It will have a different address within memory as a whole, for example, thirty thousand addresses from the beginning of memory. The latter is its absolute address.

access (AK•ses) *n.* The ability to see and change what is in a file. Anytime you tell a computer to show you a file, you are gaining access to that file. (In computer jargon, we say accessing the file.) Some files are protected so that you cannot access them unless you know a password.

access time (AK•ses TIME) *n.* The time it takes to gain access to a file. Access time for a disk file is usually short. Access time for a file on cassette tape may be longer because you have to go through all the preceding tape before you get to it.

accumulator (uh•KYOO•myuh•lay•tur) *n.* A register inside a CPU. It is an electronic device which holds one number. A second number can be brought from memory to the accumulator and added to the first number, after which the result is left in the accumulator. In some accumulators subtraction and other arithmetic operations can also be performed. All computers have an accumulator.

acoustic coupler (uh•KOO•stik KUP•lur) *n.* A device which allows a computer to "talk" over telephone lines. It has a cradle into which the telephone receiver fits. Electrical impulses from the computer go to the acoustic coupler which converts them into tones. These tones go out through the telephone receiver.

(Acoustic couplers are a kind of modem).

acronym (AK•ruh•nim) *n.* A word that is composed of the first letter or letters of other words. People who work with computers often use acronyms: for example, RAM (Random Access Memory), BASIC (Beginner's All-purpose Symbolic Instruction Code) and ASCII (American Standard Code for Information Interchange).

Some samples of acronyms:

ROM (Read Only Memory)

ASCII (American Standard Code for Information Interchange)

CODASYL (COnference for DAta SYstems Languages)

EPROM (Erasable and Programmable Read Only Memory)

FAST (Flexible Algebraic Scientific Translator)

FIFO (First In, First Out)

LISP (LISt Processing)

ALGOL (ALGOrithmic Language)

active file (AK•tiv FILE) *n.* A file that is currently in use. In some computers which many people can use at once, if a file is active (somebody is using it) no one else can use it.

ADA (AY•duh) *n.* A programming language which was developed for the Department of Defense and which many people think will be one of the most widely used languages in the 1980's and 1990's.

Here is a sample of an ADA program used to obtain square root.

```
with SQRT, SIMPLE__IO;
procedure PRINT__ROOT is
        use SIMPLE__IO;
begin
        PUT (SQRT(2.5));
end PRINT__ROOT;
```

adapter (uh•DAP•tur) *n.* A connecting device with the plug for one kind of cable and the socket for another. It is used when the cables used to connect parts of a computer do not fit each other.

add-on memory (AD-AWN MEM•uh•ree) *n*. A computer needs only a minimum amount of memory, but more memory can be added, usually in the form of extra memory chips. These are called add-on memory and allow the computer to do more than it could with less memory.

address (AD • res) *n*. A computer's memory, and the registers in its CPU, are made up of electronic devices, each of which contains data. To locate data, each device is assigned a number, which is referred to as its address.

AI (AY EYE) *n*. Abbreviation for Artificial Intelligence. A computer with AI can imitate the human ability to learn and to make decisions. No computer can do this as well as a human, although AI is improving all the time, for instance, in computers which can play chess.

ALGOL (AL•gol) *n*. An acronym for ALGOrithmic Language and the name of a programming language which is at its best doing arithmetic and logical operations.

algorithm (AL•guh•rith•um) *n*. A step-by-step procedure for solving a problem. For example, the algorithm for lighting a safety match is to tear it out of the pack, close the pack cover, and rub the match head quickly against the sandpaper strip on the pack. Most computer programs consist of algorithms, most of which are algorithms for solving mathematical problems.

alphanumeric (AL•fuh•noo•MER•ik) *adj*. Of the characters represented on a computer keyboard, those which are numbers or letters are called alphanumeric characters. Those which are punctuation or other marks are not alphanumerics.

alphanumeric data (AL•fuh•noo•MER•ik DAY•tuh) *n*. All information in the computer's memory is in the form of numbers. Even letters are represented by, that is, encoded, as numbers. The code for the letter A may be 65, the letter B may be 66, etc. The number 1 may be 49. Letters and numbers encoded in the computer are called alphanumeric data.

Code			*Code*			*Code*		
Dec.	*Hex*	*Keyboard*	*Dec.*	*Hex*	*Keyboard*	*Dec.*	*Hex*	*Keyboard*
33	21	!	52	34	4	71	47	G
34	22	"	53	35	5	72	48	H
35	23	#	54	36	6	73	49	I
36	24	$	55	37	7	74	4A	J
37	25	%	56	38	8	75	4B	K
38	26	&	57	39	9	76	4C	L
39	27	'	58	3A	:	77	4D	M
40	28	(	59	3B	;	78	4E	N
41	29	)	60	3C	<	79	4F	O
42	2A	*	61	3D	=	80	50	P
43	2B	+	62	3E	>	81	51	Q
44	2C	,	63	3F	?	82	52	R
45	2D	–	64	40	@	83	53	S
46	2E	.	65	41	A	84	54	T
47	2F	/	66	42	B	85	55	U
48	30	Ø	67	43	C	86	56	V
49	31	1	68	44	D	87	57	W
50	32	2	69	45	E	88	58	X
51	33	3	70	46	F	89	59	Y
						90	5A	Z

ALU (AY EL YOO) *n*. An abbreviation for Arithmetic and Logic Unit. This is a part of the computer, located in the Central Processing Unit. The ALU performs all commands which require that numbers be added, subtracted, multiplied or divided or that numbers be compared logically. (See logical operations.) Therefore, the ALU is one of the hardest working of all the parts of a computer.

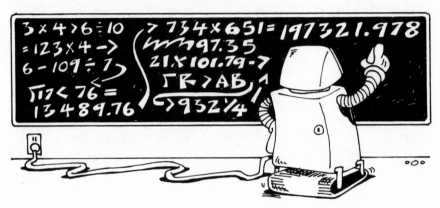

ampersand (AM•pur•sand) *n*. The character which looks like this: &. Normally, it means 'and', but in a programming language it may mean something quite different. In fact, it often may mean whatever the programmer wants it to mean.

amplifier (AM•pli•fye•ur) *n*. An electronic device which, in its simplest form, has two inputs and one output. One input is an electronic signal that carries information at a low voltage. The other input is a high voltage current that carries no information. The amplifier's output is a signal which carries the input information at the higher voltage, thus it magnifies (we say amplifies) the signal.

analog (AN•uh•lawg) *adj*. Refers to the principle of solving a problem by using a tool which operates in a way analogous to the problem. For example, the traditional watch is an analog device because the hands move around the dial analogously to the sun moving across the sky. The electronic circuits in an analog computer act analogously to the problem to be solved. Analog computers are used only for scientific and engineering problems.

analog computer (AN•uh•laug kum•PYOO•tur) *n*. A computer that represents the parts of a problem by different electrical voltages. The opposite of a digital computer.

animation (an•i•MAY•shun) *n.* Making an inanimate object or drawing appear to move by rapidly displaying a series of pictures of it, each one in a slightly different position. Some computers can take a picture and automatically make it appear to move in certain ways. This is a form of animation sometimes called pseudo-animation.

ANSI (AN•see) *n.* Acronym for American National Standards Institute. This organization, located in New York City, coordinates and publicizes voluntary standards for a wide range of industries, including the computer industry.

apostrophe (uh•POS•truh•fee) *n.* The character on a computer keyboard which looks like this: '. In a programming language an apostrophe might have some special meaning.

application program (ap•li•KAY•shun PROH•gram) *n.* A computer program that is applied to tasks outside of the computer. For example, a word-processing program, or a program to balance your checkbook are application programs.

argument (AHR•gyoo•ment) *n.* In many programming languages, some commands require one or more arguments, which are numbers that tell the computer how to use that command. For example, the BASIC command PLOT tells the computer to draw a point on the screen, but it requires two arguments to locate where that point should be.

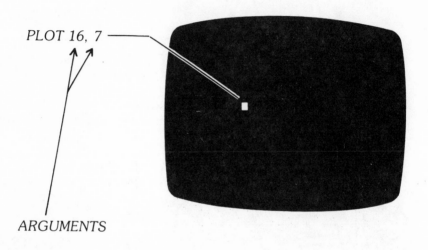

PLOT 16, 7

ARGUMENTS

arithmetic operation (uh•RITH•muh•tic op•uh•RAY•shun) *n.* One of the following four operations, which all computers can perform: addition, subtraction, multiplication and division.

arithmetic-logic unit (uh• RITH•muh•tic LOJ•ic YOO•nit)*n.* The same as ALU.

array (uh•RAY) *n.* A section of a computer's memory set aside to store certain information. Think of an array as a number of blocks, each one holding a unit of information. An array may be two-dimensional, in which case these blocks are arranged in rows and columns, like a checker board, so that each block may be located by a row number and a column number. However, some arrays have only one row, and some arrays have more than two dimensions.

artificial intelligence (ahr•ti•FISH•ul in•TEL•i•jence) *n.* Same as AI.

ASCII (AS•kee) *n.* Acronym for American Standard Code for Information Interchange. ASCII is the code in which a number is assigned to each character on a computer keyboard. Most computers use the ASCII code.

assembler (uh•SEM•bler) *n.* A program which translates a program written in assembly language into machine language which the computer can understand. Each assembly language instruction is translated into one machine language instruction.

assembly language (uh•SEM•blee LANG•gwij) *n.* A programming language in which each command in the instruction set is represented by a word. These words are easier to remember than the machine code of the instruction. For example, the instruction for a jump might be JMP in assembly language.

This particular routine checks whether a character has been typed on the keyboard, waits until one is typed and then puts that letter or number on the screen.

Ø3B1	F6	EF	F4	LDB
Ø3B4	C5	Ø2		BITB
Ø3B6	27	F9		BEQ
Ø3B8	84	7F		ANDA
Ø3BA	B7	EF	F5	STA
Ø3BD	39			RTS

assignment statement (uh•SINE•ment STATE•ment) *n.* A statement which tells the computer to assign a value to a given variable. For example, the BASIC statement, LET A = 2, tells the computer that whenever it meets the letter A in the program, it should act as if it were the number 2.

asterisk (AS•tuh•risk) *n.* On a computer keyboard, the character which looks like this: ✱ . In a program, an asterisk may have a special meaning.

19

asynchronous (ay•SING•kruh•nus) *adj.* Working so that each operation's conclusion is a signal for the next operation to begin. The opposite of synchronous, in which operations begin on the beats of a clock, so that sometimes an operation ends some time before the next one begins.

authoring language (AW•thur•ing LANG•gwij) *n.* A programming language used to write educational programs. For example, if a teacher wanted to program a computer to teach simple arithmetic, she would use an authoring language. PILOT is a well-known language that was designed for authoring.

A program written in PILOT looks like this:

```
1Ø  R: CONDITIONAL MATCH PROGRAM
2Ø  T: WHO WAS THE 16TH PRESIDENT OF THE UNITED STATES?
3Ø  A: $P
4Ø  M: ABRAHAM LINCOLN, LINCOLN, ABE LINCOLN
5Ø  TY: RIGHT! GOOD FOR YOU.
6Ø  TN: NO, THE ANSWER IS ABRAHAM LINCOLN.
7Ø  T: COME BACK LATER FOR ANOTHER PRESIDENT QUESTION.
8Ø  E:
```

automation (aw•toh•MAY•shun) *n.* The use of machines to do work. Computers have made much more automation possible. A recent example of computerized automation is robots which can weld cars, something which only a few years ago could only be done by a person.

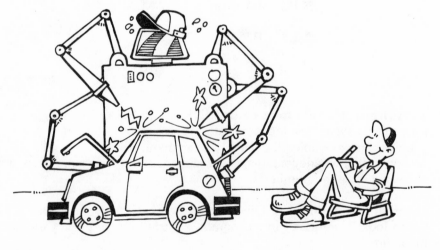

backslash (BAK•slash) *n.* On a computer keyboard, the character which looks like this: \ . In a program, a backslash may have a special meaning.

backspace key (BAK•spays KEE) *n.* The key on a computer keyboard which, when pressed, makes the cursor move backwards one space. Usually, the backspace key is marked with an arrow pointing to the left.

backup (BAK•up) *n.* A copy of some information which you can use if the original is lost or damaged. With "soft" information that can be erased, like data on a disk or cassette tape, keeping a backup is very important.

bar code (BAR KOHD) *n.* The vertical black stripes which you have seen on many products. Each stripe stands for a different number or letter. A special attachment lets a computer read these bar codes, which often tell what a product's price is.

bar code reader (BAR KOHD REE•dur) *n.* A special device which is attached to a computer so that the computer can read bar codes. Bar code readers use lenses and reflected light to convert the bar code into numbers and letters.

base (BAYS) *n.* Refers to numbering systems. People normally use a base ten numbering system, with ten digits, zero through 9. Computers, however, use a base two, or binary system which has only zero and one as digits. Programmers often use octal (base eight) and hexadecimal, or hex (base 16) numbering systems.

base eight (BAYS AYT) *n.* A numbering system which uses only eight digits, zero through seven. The number eight in base eight is written 10 (one eight plus zero). Base eight is also called octal.

base sixteen (BAYS SIKS•TEEN) *n.* A numbering system which uses sixteen digits, zero through nine, plus the letters A through F. The number ten in base sixteen is written A. The number sixteen is written 10. The number thirty is written 1E (one sixteen plus fourteen). Base sixteen is also called hex or hexadecimal.

base ten (BAYS TEN) *n.* The numbering system we normally use. It has ten digits, zero through nine, and the number ten is written 10 (one ten plus zero). We probably use base ten because humans began counting on their fingers.

base two (BAYS TOO) *n.* A numbering system which uses only two digits, zero and one. The number two in base two is written 10 (one two plus zero). The number three is written 11. Base two is the numbering system in which a computer "thinks", since the electrical signals in a computer are either high voltage (one) or no voltage (zero). Base two is also called binary.

BASIC (BAY•sik) *n.* Acronym for Beginner's All-purpose Symbolic Instruction Code. BASIC is a programming language that is relatively easy to use and was originally developed for use in teaching beginning programmers. Now it is also used for some serious programming.

Here is a sample program in BASIC that prints the multiples of 5 from 0 to 100.

```
10 HOME
20 A = 0
30 PRINT A,
40 GOSUB 100
50 IF A = 100 THEN 80
60 A = A + 5
70 GOTO 30
80 END

100 FOR T = 1 TO 250
110 NEXT T
120 RETURN
```

batch processing (BATCH PROS•es•ing) *n.* Running a program in a manner which does not allow the user to communicate with the computer once the program starts to run. Some computer programs are written on a sequence of punched cards. The programmer submits a "batch" of cards to the computer and comes back later for the results.

baud rate (BAWD RAYT) *n.* Refers to the speed at which an electronic communication travels through a line. For example, a computer sending data over the telephone lines may send it at 300 baud, which is slow, or 9600 baud, which is fast. Baud is not necessarily the same as bits per second. The term comes from the name of J.M.E. Baudot, who invented a signalling code that was adopted by the French telegraph system in 1877.

binary (BI·nuh·ree) *adj.* Same as base two.

binary code (BI·nuh·ree KOHD) *n.* A code in which characters are represented by patterns of ones and zeros. For example, the binary number 1000001 (65 in base 10) might stand for the letter A.

Decimal   Binary

$$0 = 0\ 0\ 0\ 0\ 0\ 0\ 0$$
$$1 = 0\ 0\ 0\ 0\ 0\ 0\ 1$$
$$2 = 0\ 0\ 0\ 0\ 0\ 1\ 0$$
$$10 = 0\ 0\ 0\ 0\ 1\ 0\ 1\ 0$$
$$50 = 0\ 0\ 1\ 1\ 0\ 0\ 1\ 0$$
$$72 = 0\ 1\ 0\ 0\ 1\ 0\ 0\ 0$$
$$225 = 1\ 1\ 1\ 0\ 0\ 0\ 1$$
$$255 = 1\ 1\ 1\ 1\ 1\ 1\ 1\ 1$$

bit (BIT) *n.* An acronym for BInary uniT. A bit is one digit in a binary number; that is, either a one or a zero.

black box (BLAK BOKS) *n.* A jargon term used, often jokingly, by people in the electronics field. Generally, it means any electronic component that plugs into a computer (or other system) to perform a specific function.

HERE'S YOUR BLACK BOX

blank (BLANGK) *v.* A picture (or text) on a video screen is the result of a beam of electrons that hit the phosphorescent screen, causing it to glow. This beam scans the screen from top to bottom, one line at a time, also scanning each line from the viewer's left to right. It takes a brief time for the beam to move from the end of one line to the beginning of the next, or from the bottom of the screen back to the top, to start the next scan. During this time, the beam is turned off, or blanked, to avoid interfering with the picture on the screen.

block (BLOK) *n.* A chunk of memory. For example, in word processing, each character is stored in one memory location, and a paragraph, say, is stored in a block of memory.

board (BOHRD) *n.* Short for printed circuit board, a piece of material that does not conduct electricity, usually some kind of plastic. Electrical components such as chips, resistors, capacitors, etc. are soldered on the board. These components are connected not by wires, but by strips of metal printed onto the surface of the board.

boolean (BOO•lee•un) *adj.* A branch of mathematical logic named after its inventor, George Boole. Boolean logic is a set of rules which allow logical relations to be described in mathematical terms. For example, in boolean terms, one stands for true, zero stands for false. The statement, "A truth and a falsehood together are a falsehood" would be $1 \times 0 = 0$.

boot (BOOT) *v*. Taken from the term boot-strap. When a computer is first turned on, it cannot do anything by itself. A computer only does things when given a command. To boot the computer means to load a program which will in turn allow it to obey commands or other programs. Sometimes the program is booted automatically when the computer is turned on.

branch (BRANCH) *v*. Often a program will direct the computer to do one thing under certain conditions and otherwise to do something else. We say that this is a branching in the program flow. The computer will follow one line of action or will branch off into another.

branching (BRANCH•ing) *n*. A program or set of instructions which cause the computer's activity to branch, or which contain branching structures.

bubble memory (BUBL MEM•uh•ree) *n*. An advanced method for storing information. Bits of information are stored magnetically on a thin metallic film that is deposited on a slice of garnet. Bubble memory promises to store much more information in a given space than methods currently in use, such as metal oxide tapes and disks.

buffer (BUF•ur) *n.* A place where data may be stored temporarily. This may be a reserved section of memory or a printed circuit board with its own memory used only as a buffer.

bug (BUG) *n.* A mistake or omission which causes a program or an electronic device to operate incorrectly. Generally, bugs are imperfections which can be fixed without having to change the overall design.

bus (BUS) *n.* A path for signals which are sent and received by components inside a computer. A component sends a signal onto a bus, and only the component to which it is addressed receives the signal, although other components are also connected to the bus. All microcomputers have three busses, the address bus, the data bus and the control bus.

byte (BITE) *n.* The number of bits that are necessary to represent the code for one alphabetic character. Most commonly, a byte is eight bits long.

Character	Code
A	01000001
$	00100100
)	00101001
<	00111100
F	01000110
Z	01011010

CAI (CEE•AY•EYE) *n*. Abbreviation for Computer Assisted (or Aided) Instruction. This is a very general term for all the ways in which computers might help to teach.

calculator (KAL•kyuh•lay•tur) *n*. A small electronic device which performs mathematical operations automatically. The difference between a calculator and a computer is that the calculator can manipulate numbers; the computer also manipulates numbers, but the numbers can stand for other things, like text or pictures.

call (KAWL) *n*. A kind of instruction. A call instruction tells a computer to execute a series of other instructions which are already in the computer's memory, beginning at a location which the user specifies when he gives the call instruction.

canned program (KAND PROH•gram) *n.* A jargon term for a program which is sold as is, rather than designed for a specific customer, like a pair of off-the-rack trousers. Usually canned programs serve general rather than specific purposes, and the maker will not customize the program.

card reader (KAHRD REE•dur) *n.* Cards may be marked by having holes punched in them or by having the holes filled in with pencil. A device which converts the markings on a card into an electronic signal is called a card reader. When a card reader is connected to a computer, information from the marked cards can be used by the computer.

carriage return key (return key) (KAIR•ij ri•TURN KEE) *n.* On a keyboard, the key which is used to make the cursor move to the beginning of the next line on the display screen. In text processing, the carriage return key marks the end of a paragraph. The key is usually marked with an arrow with a bent tail, or by the word 'return' or the word 'enter'.

cartridge (KAHR•trij) *n.* A container which holds a tape that a computer can read. Microcomputer cartridge tapes hold less information than cassettes or disks and usually plug into a receptacle on the microcomputer. (A disk cartridge, used on larger computers, is a hard disk that can be removed and replaced in a large device which transfers information between the disk and the computer.)

cassette (kuh•SET) *n.* A container, usually made of plastic, in which is a tape that a computer can read. The cassette can be inserted into a cassette player, which is a separate device from the computer. If the player is connected to a computer, the information on the tape can be entered into the computer.

cassette recorder (kuh•SET ri•KOR•dur) *n.* A device which is used to record information on a cassette. Usually, the same device both records and plays a cassette tape. When it is connected to a computer, information from the computer can be recorded onto the tape, and information from the tape can be entered into the computer.

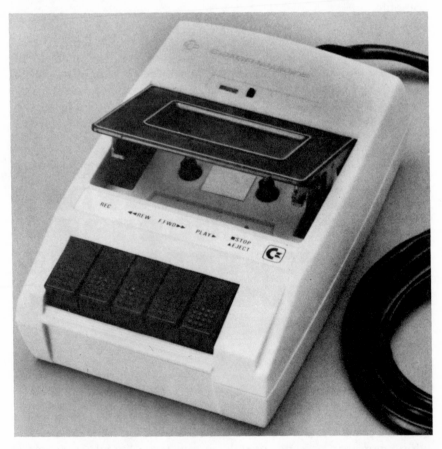

cassette tape (kuh•SET TAYP) *n.* The tape, usually an eighth of an inch wide, which is used in a cassette. It is the same as tape used for audio recordings, but computer information can also be recorded on it.

cathode ray tube (CRT) (KATH•ohd RAY TOOB) *n.* The part of a television or monitor which forms the picture. It consists of a large vacuum tube, a phosphorescent screen, a device which sends a narrow beam of electrons toward the screen, and a magnet which controls the direction of the electron beam. The term is also used to mean any monitor which uses a CRT to produce a display of text or pictures.

central processing unit (SEN•trul PROS•es•ing YOO•nit) *n.* Same as central processor.

central processor (SEN•trul PROS•es•ur) *n.* The most important part of a computer. The central processor executes instructions and manipulates numbers and controls the computer's other operations. In a microcomputer, all the parts of the central processor are located on one chip called the microprocessor. A computer system consists of the central processor, memory and peripheral devices. (Sometimes memory is considered a part of the central processor.)

channel (CHANL) *n.* A route taken by information travelling from one device or part of a device to another. In computers, a channel usually means a special unit dedicated to transferring information. The capacity of a channel (the amount of information it can carry) is usually given in bytes (or kilobytes) per second.

character set (KAIR•ik•tur SET) *n*. The characters which a computer can use. For example, a character set of 96 characters might consist of 32 control characters, digits 0 through 9, capital letters A through Z, one blank space and 27 punctuation and other marks.

chip (CHIP) *n*. A jargon term which can mean either an integrated circuit on a silicon chip, or the carrier in which the chip is located. A carrier is a block with several metal pins that can be plugged into a receptacle on a printed circuit board. Carriers are usually black.

circuit (SUR•kit) *n*. In electronics, a circuit is any combination of conductors and electronic devices through which electricity can pass. An electrical circuit may be miles long, in the case of utility power lines, yards long in the case of home wiring, inches in the case of a printed circuit board, or microscopic in the case of an integrated circuit.

closed loop (KLOHZD LOOP) *n.* In programming, a series of instructions which the computer executes over and over again, like a stuck record, because the last instruction tells the computer to go back and start the series over again. Usually this is caused by a mistake in the program. A closed loop can also be a job which the computer does without human interference, because the computer can tell when conditions change and change its own actions accordingly. For example, if a computer attached to a thermostat turns a heater on and off depending on the temperature, we say that the computer, the thermostat and the heater form a closed loop.

COBOL (KOH •bohl) *n.* Acronym for COmmon Business Oriented Language. A programming language developed for and widely used in business.

Here is a portion of a COBOL version of a payroll program:

DATA DIVISION
FILE SECTION
FD CARD FILE   LABEL RECORD IS OMITTED

```
01 TIME CARD
02 FILLER               PICTURE X (5).
02 IN-EMPLOYEE-NAME     PICTURE X (15).
02 IN-INITIALS          PICTURE X (2).
02 FILLER               PICTURE X (8).
02 IN-HOURS-WORKED      PICTURE 99V9.
02 FILLER               PICTURE X (7).
02 IN-PAY-RATE          PICTURE 99V99.
02 FILLER               PICTURE X (36).
```

code (KOHD) *n.* Generally, any set of characters that stand for different characters. For example, the ASCII code in which each character on the keyboard is represented by a number. Every programming language is a code in which characters stand for different combinations of ones and zeros (machine language). Therefore, we refer to the written lines of a program as lines of code.

column (KOL•um) *n.* When you work with computers, it is often convenient to reduce a large field of information into smaller units. This is done by dividing the large field into horizontal strips called rows and vertical strips called columns. Examples are two dimensional arrays and monitor screens. Once divided into strips, the crossing strips form boxes, as on a checker board. Each box can then be identified by the number of its row and its column.

command (kuh•MAND) *n.* Loosely, the same thing as 'instruction'. Properly, a command is one of two things. A command can be an electronic impulse which tells the computer to do something, as distinct from a written instruction. Also, most instructions have several parts. For example, an ADD instruction may tell a computer to add, and then tell it what numbers to add and where in the computer to put those numbers. The part of the instruction that just tells it to add is also called the command.

comment (KOM•ent) *n.* A note, written in English, which is part of a program and explains and clarifies what that program does. Special characters accompanying such notes tell the computer to ignore them; they are for humans only.

communications (kuh•myoo•ni•KAY•shuns) *n.* In the computer world, communications generally refers to sending information to or from a computer which may be in the next room or on the other side of the world, or even in a lunar lander on the moon.

communications satellite (kuh•myoo•ni•KAY•shuns SA•tuh•lite) *n.* A satellite in orbit hundreds of miles above the earth, used to receive information from one station on earth and send it back to another station elsewhere on earth. For many reasons, it is better to send some information through communications satellites than by radio waves or wires over land.

compiler (kum•PILE•ur) *n.* A program that translates another program written in high level language into a machine language version which a computer can understand. Each high level instruction is translated into one or more machine language instructions. The result is a complete program that may be run anytime without ever being compiled again.

compute (kum•PYOOT) *v.* To receive data, change it in obedience to organized instructions, and give back the results. These results may be new information or electronic signals used to control machines.

computer (kum•PYOO•tur) *n.* A machine which can compute.

computer art (kum•PYOO•tur AHRT) *n*. Pictures, or graphics, which are produced for artistic reasons using a computer. The final work may be in the form of a monitor display, a print on paper, a photographic or videotape image.

computer graphics (kum•PYOO•tur GRAF•iks) *n*. Pictures, charts, plans, designs, animation or any other display, including text characters, created using a computer's ability to draw and color shapes. (Computers also produce text characters which are not graphics.)

computer language (kum•PYOO•tur LANG•gwij) *n*. Any code which is used to write instructions that a computer will obey. This includes machine language, assembly language and high level languages. The term means the same as 'programming language'.

computer literacy (kum•PYOO•tur LIT•ur•ruh•see) *n*. Having a general idea about how computers work, what they can and cannot do, and how to use them.

computer operator (kum•PYOO•tur OP•uh•ray•tur) *n*. A computer operator may be either of two things. One is any human who operates a computer. The other is the part of an instruction to a computer which tells it what operation to perform.

computer output (kum•PYOO•tur OWT•puut) *n*. Data communicated from a computer. This may be the result of an operation sent to a monitor to be displayed, text sent to a printer to be typed, data sent to a modem to be transmitted over the phone lines, or any other data going out from a computer.

computer program (kum•PYOO•tur PROH•gram) *n*. A series of instructions which the computer will follow. Each program is designed to cause the computer to perform a specific task or solve a specific problem. Without a program, computers can do nothing.

Here is a sample computer program in Apple BASIC whose printout has varied speeds.

```
NEW
1Ø HOME
2Ø SPEED = 1ØØ
3Ø PRINT "THE RABBIT GOES"
4Ø SPEED = 255
5Ø PRINT
6Ø PRINT "F . . . . . A . . . . . S . . . . . T"
7Ø PRINT: PRINT: PRINT
8Ø SPEED = 1ØØ
9Ø PRINT "THE TURTLE GOES"
1ØØ SPEED = Ø
11Ø PRINT
12Ø PRINT "S . . . . . L . . . . . O . . . . . W"
13Ø SPEED = 255
14Ø END
```

computer science (kum•PYOO•tur SYE•unce) *n*. The study of how computers handle information and of ways to improve information handling methods in the future. Thirty years ago computer science scarcely existed, and now it is a very large field taught at almost all colleges and universities.

computer system (kum•PYOO•tur SIS•tum) *n.* A central processing unit and the peripheral devices connected to it, for example, a monitor, a printer, a disk drive. That is, a computer system is a group of electronic devices which work together not only to process data, but to communicate data to and from the outside world.

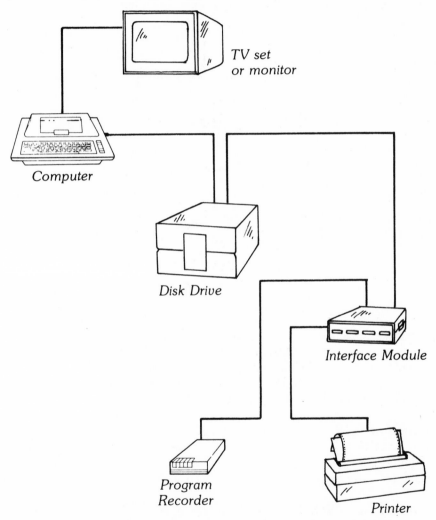

TV set
or monitor

Computer

Disk Drive

Interface Module

Program
Recorder

Printer

concatenate (kon•KAT•uh•nayt) *v.* To link things together in a chain. For example, the two words "draw" and "bridge" could be concatenated into the word "drawbridge". Or two files of information in a computer's memory can be concatenated into one larger file.

conditional branch (kun•DISH•un•ul BRANCH) *n.* A program may tell a computer to do one of several things. Which one it does depends on some condition. For example, if a statement is true, do one thing, if it is false do something else, and if its truth is unknown do a third thing. The computer will follow one of these three branches, depending on the condition of the statement's truth. This is called a conditional branch.

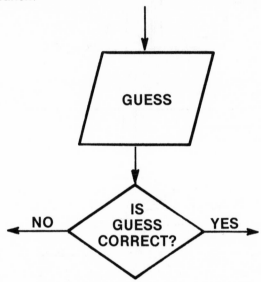

console (KON•sohl) *n.* The part of a computer where humans may enter and receive information. This is usually a keyboard and a monitor, but instead of a keyboard, it may have a number of switches to enter information in code, and information may come out not to a monitor, but on paper instead.

constant (KON•stunt) *n.* A symbol which always has the same value. For example, in a program, whenever the computer encounters the letter X, if it must treat the X as if it were the number 18, we say X is a constant. The opposite of a constant is a variable.

control (kun•TROHL) *n.*, *v.* Computers are said to operate under the *control* of a program. Computer operation is said to be controlled by the central processing unit. Peripheral devices are said to be controlled by their own circuitry in response to signals from the central processing unit. In short, whenever a program or a device provides information which tells another device what to do, it is said to control it.

control characters (kun•TROHL KAIR•ik•turs) *n*. Characters which, when entered at the keyboard, send commands to the computer instead of code for a text character. Usually, the keyboard has a key marked CTRL, called the control key. Control characters are formed by pressing the control key and another key at the same time. Control character operations include ringing the computer bell, performing a carriage return, moving a cursor on the monitor screen, or whatever operation a program might define.

control clock (kun•TROHL KLOCK) *n*. An electronic device inside a computer which emits a periodic signal. Computer operations are performed in step with the very rapid "beats" of this signal. Usually, it is simply called the clock.

control unit (kun•TROHL YOO•nit) *n*. This term has two meanings. One is that part of the central processing unit which supervises the execution of a program, telling each part of the computer when to do something. Also, control unit can mean any electronic circuitry that controls the operation of a peripheral device.

core (KOHR) *n*. The main memory of a computer, as distinct from mass storage. The term comes from a kind of memory device which stored electrical charges in metal cores. Cores are not used as much anymore, but the name has stuck, mostly for very large computers.

counter (KOWN•tur) *n*. Any part of a computer used to keep track of how many times something has happened. For example, a computer may be connected to a turnstile, and every time someone goes through the turnstile, the computer may add one to the number in a memory location. That memory location is being used as a counter.

CPU (SEE PEE YOO) *n.* Abbreviation for Central Processing Unit.

cursor (KUR•sur) *n.* A small shape used to mark the position on a monitor screen where information may be entered. In a word processor, the cursor marks the position where the next character will be typed, and each time a key is hit, the cursor moves one position. A cursor may be a flashing rectangle, an underscore line, or some other shape.

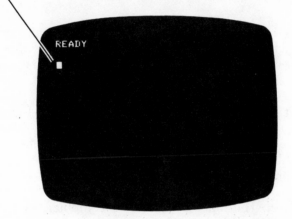

daisy wheel printer (DAY•zee WEEL PRIN•tur) *n*. A daisy wheel consists of a round center from which a number of short strips stick out, like the petals on a daisy. One keyboard character is placed on each petal. The printer types characters by rapidly turning the daisy wheel so that the correct character is lined up in front of the ribbon, and then striking it against the paper.

data (DAY•tuh) *n*. Any collection of symbols, such as letters, numbers or other characters. Each datum carries so little information that it is meaningless by itself, like a single letter. Data are manipulated by a computer and arranged into groups which convey meaning.

data bank (DAY•tuh BANGK) *n*. A file or files kept in a computer's mass storage. Each file in a data bank contains a wide variety of information on a single subject. For example, the federal government may keep a data bank on public health in which for every person in the country a file exists containing that person's medical history.

data base (DAY•tuh BAYS) *n*. A way of organizing information kept in a computer's mass storage. Each file is divided into fields, and each field is divided into records. No matter what information is in the files, any piece of information may be found in a certain field , within a certain record within a certain file. Many programs may share a data base, some putting information into it, some taking it out, and some doing both.

data processing (DAY•tuh PROS•es•ing) *n*. What goes on inside a computer. Text, numbers, pictures or other information is converted into data and that data is processed; i.e., re-organized, added to, deleted, or changed from one form to another.

debug (DEE•bug) *v*. To remove bugs (mistakes) from a program or from the design of a hardware system.

debugging aids (DEE•bug•ing AYDZ) *n*. Programs which make it easier to find the bugs in a program. These include programs which let you execute a program one instruction at a time, let you see the contents of CPU registers while the program runs, or display the line number of each instruction that is executed.

decimal system (DES•uh•mul SIS•tum) *n*. Same as base ten.

decode (dee•KOHD) *v.* To translate data that is written in computer code into a form which humans can understand.

decrement (DEK•ruh•ment) *v.* To decrease the value of a number. For example, a program designed to count the number of tires in a warehouse would set aside a memory location to hold the number of tires. Every time a tire was shipped out of the warehouse, the computer would decrement that number.

decrypt (dee•KRIPT) *v.* To break the code used in secret messages, a task for which computers are extremely useful. The military and intelligence agencies use computers in decryption.

default (di•FAWLT) *v.* A value automatically selected by a computer unless a user selects some other value. For instance, a word processor might allow the user to set page margins at any value, but if he makes no selection, the margins will default to a width of twelve characters.

deferred mode(di•FURD MOHD) *n.* A sequence of instructions (a program) may be typed into a computer's memory, and/or stored on disk or tape, and executed later. This is called deferred mode, as distinct from immediate mode in which one instruction at a time is sent to the computer from a keyboard or other input device, and executed immediately.

degauss (dee•GOWS) *v.* To demagnetize. In computers, information is erased from magnetic tape with a strong electromagnet called a deguasser.

delay (di•LAY) *v.* To cause an electronic signal to slow down or to halt briefly. This is done in computers in a number of ways for a variety of reasons.

demagnetize (dee•MAG•nuh•tize) *v.* Magnetic media like tapes or disks are covered with thin films containing tiny particles of iron. When any of these particles are magnetized they all point in one direction. Demagnetization rearranges the particles so that they all point in different directions.

device (di•VICE) *n.* In computers, a device, or peripheral device, is a piece of equipment located outside of the CPU with which the CPU communicates through input and output ports. Examples of devices are printers, card readers, disk drives and cassette players.

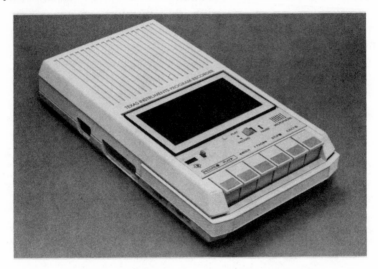

diagnostics (dye•ag•NOS•tiks) *n.* Procedures used to identify and locate bugs and other malfunctions in a piece of equipment.

digital (DI•ji•tuhl) *adj.* Breaking down things into tiny parts which can be represented by numbers. For example, the peaks and valleys of a mountain range might be connected with a continuous wavy line. But that line could be broken down into points a foot apart, each with its own elevation. The line outline of the mountain range could be reconstructed from a list of all these elevations, expressed as numbers.

digital computer (DI•ji•tuhl kum•PYOO•tur) *n.* A computer which works by breaking down every problem or task into parts that can be represented by numbers, and then manipulating the numbers to solve the problem and perform the task. The opposite of analog computer.

digitizer (DI•ji•tize•ur) *n.* A device which converts analog information into a digital form. For instance, a digitizer might convert a signal from a television camera into a series of numbers. Those numbers could be stored in a computer. The computer could then use those numbers to recreate a picture of whatever the camera had been pointed at.

digits (DI•jits) *n.* Numbers. For example, in the decimal system, we use the digits zero through nine.

directory (di•REK•tor•ree) *n.* In computers, a list of files kept in mass storage, along with their contents. A computer user can look at the directory to see what information he has in the files currently available to him.

disk, hard (DISK, HAHRD) *n.* One kind of mass storage is the disk. It is thin, flat and covered with a film of magnetic material on which data can be recorded. Hard disks are made of rigid plastic and can hold much more data than floppy disks.

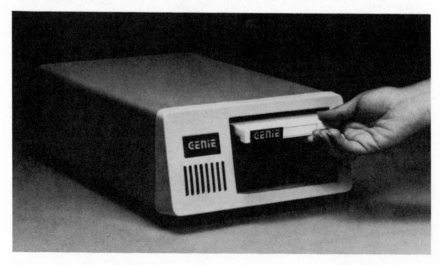

disk drive (DISK DRIVE) *n.* A device which can transfer data to and from a disk and send that data to and from a computer to which it is connected. Disk drives for floppy disks have slots in front into which the floppy disk can be inserted. Some hard disk drives contain permanent disks which cannot be removed. Large computers use hard disk drives which contain several disks arranged one above the other.

disk operating system (DOS) (DISK OP•uh•rayt•ing SIS•tum) *n.* A program or programs which control communication and transfer of data between a computer and its disk drive (or drives). A typical DOS does things like keep the directory in order, tell the disk drive when to send data and when to receive it, tell the disk drive which file on the disk data is supposed to go to or come from, put special signals on a disk to keep track of where data is located on it, and many other functions.

diskette (disk•ET) *n.* A floppy disk which is five and one quarter inches (13.34 cm) in diameter.

display (di•SPLAY) *n*. Any visible data coming directly from a computer. Text or pictures on a monitor are examples of computer displays. The same data printed on paper would not be a display.

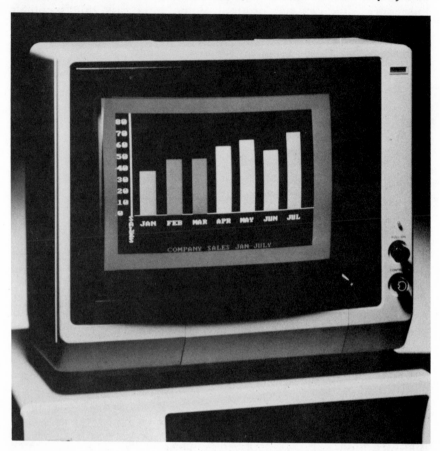

document (DOK•yuh•ment) *n*. Any communication written on paper in human language, such as English. A document may be a business letter, a diagram of electronic circuitry, or a user's manual for a computer program.

documentation (dok•yuh•men•TAY•shun) *n*. This term has two meanings. One is the written explanations and instructions which come with a computer program or a piece of equipment to help a human use it. The other meaning is the comments which are part of a program, written by the programmer for humans, to help them understand what the program code stands for.

dot matrix printer (DOT MAY•triks PRIN•tur) *n*. A printer which can print groups of tiny dots on a piece of paper. These dots may be arranged into the shape of alphabet letters. They also may be arranged to create a picture, like the tiny dots in newspaper photographs. Dot matrix printers may be used to print both text and graphics.

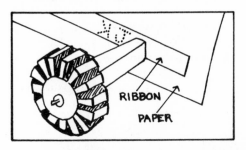

RIBBON

PAPER

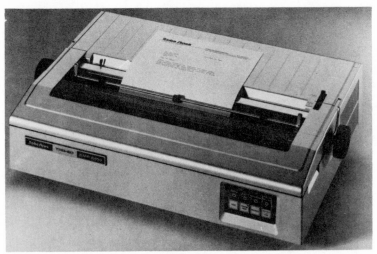

download (DOWN•lohd) *v*. To transfer a file or block of data from a large computer to a smaller one. Sometimes this term is used to mean transfer of data from any computer to any other. If the two computers are different models or makes, downloading might require some alterations to the data after it is received, to make the data understandable to the receiving computer.

down time (DOWN TIME) *n*. A jargon term for the time during which a computer is turned off because something is wrong with it, it is receiving maintenance, it is being modified or for some other reason it is not usable.

dump (DUMP) *v*. To transfer all the data located in a section of memory from a computer to some peripheral device. The difference between a dump and other kinds of data transfer is that a dump is concerned more with a certain part of memory than with a certain body of data.

dynamic memory (dye•NAM•ik MEM•uh•ree) *n*. Computer memory is divided into cells. Each cell holds one bit of data. Dynamic memory only holds data for a short time, and then loses it. Computers with dynamic memory constantly copy the content of each cell and send it back to the cell before it is lost. This is called refreshing the memory.

edit (ED·it) *v*. To change information. Two examples are, first, to revise a document by adding, deleting or moving words, and second, to change a drawing by adding, deleting or moving lines or other parts of the objects drawn.

editor (ED·i·tur) *n*. In computers, any program, machine, or combination of the two that lets you edit something.

eighty-column card (AY·tee KOL·um KAHRD) *n*. A printed circuit board which can be plugged into a microcomputer so that its video display is expanded from forty columns across to eighty columns across. Better word processors use an eighty column format because a typed page usually is more than forty characters across.

electrical impulses (i•LEK•tri•kul IM•pul•sez) *n.* One way to make an electrical current carry data is to vary its voltage. For example, a current at seven volts may stand for a one, and a current at zero volts may be zero. Electrical circuits can be made so that the current moving in them changes between, say, seven volts and no volts. Each of these changes is called an impulse.

electronic (i•lek•TRON•ik) *adj.* A term that is used loosely to mean anything that uses electronic amplifiers such as vacuum tubes, transistors or integrated circuits. Examples are calculators, computers, control systems for anything from radar to microwave ovens, televisions, radio and so on. The term also may mean a job that used to be done mechanically but now is done with electronics, such as printing, typing or drafting.

electronic printing (i•lek•TRON•ic PRIN•ting) *n.* This may mean either of two things. One is printing in which the manual setting of type, and other jobs, are done automatically by electronic equipment. The other is using a printer connected to a computer to type documents or graphics.

ENIAC (EE•nee•ak) *n.* Acronym for Electronic Numerical Integrator And Calculator, the first electronic computer. It was built between 1943 and 1946 using vacuum tubes. It was as large as a small room and could do less than today's microcomputers.

enter (EN•tur) *v.* To send information from a keyboard, panel switch or other device, directly to the computer. When a user gives a command to the computer, we say the command is entered when the user hits the RETURN key.

EPROM (EE•prom) *n.* Acronym for Erasable and Programmable Read Only Memory. A kind of memory chip which stores certain information whether the computer is on or off. This information can be erased by exposure to ultraviolet light and new information can be stored in the chip.

erase (i•RACE) *v.* To remove data from memory. This can be main memory, inside the computer, or mass storage such as a disk or tape.

error (AIR•ur) *n*. A mistake in a program or made by a user. Such a mistake prevents a computer from performing some operation. Often, but not always, the computer will display a message describing the error so that it may be corrected.

ESC (EE ESS CEE) *n*. Abbreviation often used to label the escape key on a computer keyboard.

escape key (e•SKAYP KEE) *n*. A key on many computer keyboards. A program can use this key to do anything the programmer wants it to do. However, it usually is used to take control of the computer away from a program, or to escape from that program.

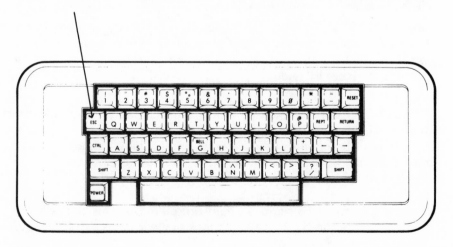

exclamation point (ek•skla•MAY•shun POINT) *n.* The keyboard character which looks like this: !. In a program, it can have special meanings, one of which is to store data in a memory location.

execute (EK•si•kyoot) *v.* Obey an instruction or list of instructions. Thus we say that a computer executes a program.

face (FACE) *n.* The printed side of a punched card.

```
CODED WITH ALL THE WORDS OF THE SENTENCE IN THIS PARAGRAPH.
```

facsimile (fak•SIM•i•lee) *n.* Converting a picture into an electronic signal that can be transmitted to a distant location where the picture can be reconstructed. Also called fax.

fault (FAWLT) *n.* A failure in a piece of hardware that prevents it from performing a task. This can be trivial, such as a printer running out of paper, or serious, such as a power supply going dead.

ferrous oxide (FER•us OK•side) *n.* The substance which coats recording tape and disks. Since it has iron in it, it can be magnetized. Therefore, data may be recorded on it magnetically.

field (FEELD) *n.* The most detailed unit of information storage. A file is divided into records and a record is divided into fields. For example, a data base about life on Earth may contain one file on animals with four legs. This may include a record on giraffes, a record on horses, a record on crocodiles and so on. The record on each of these animals may include fields on height, weight, habitat, or kinds of food.

file (FILE) *n.* Information stored by a computer is divided into files in the same way that information on paper is divided into files in a file drawer. Each file holds information on a general heading.

firmware (FURM•wair) *n.* Data stored in Read Only Memory, usually as part of a printed circuit board which can be plugged into a computer. Since it contains information (software) but consists of circuitry (hardware), it has been given the name firmware.

flag (FLAG) *n.* A small amount of memory, usually one byte or one bit, which is used to indicate if a certain condition, or which one of several conditions, is in effect. For example, a computer used to control a heater may be connected to a thermostat. Whenever the temperature exceeded 68° F (20°C) the computer might change the value in a memory location from zero to one. That memory location might be called a sixty-eight (twenty) degree flag. Whenever the sixty -eight (twenty) degree flag was set to one, the computer might turn off the heater.

floating point arithmetic (FLOHT•ing POINT uh•RITH•muh•tik) *n.* Arithmetic operations (addition, subtraction, multiplication, division) which can handle accurately numbers containing decimal points.

floppy disk (FLOP•ee DISK) *n.* One kind of mass storage is the disk. It is thin, flat and covered with a film of magnetic material on which data can be recorded. Floppy disks are made of thin plastic and can bend easily. The original floppy disks were eight inches (20.32 cm) in diameter, but now all flexible disks are called floppy disks.

flowchart (FLOH•chahrt) *n.* A special kind of diagram used to show how a computer program works. It consists of boxes labeled with each function that the program performs. The boxes are connected by lines which illustrate the sequence in which functions are performed. Different kinds of functions are put in differently shaped boxes; for example, all functions in which the computer decides among different courses of action are diamond shaped.

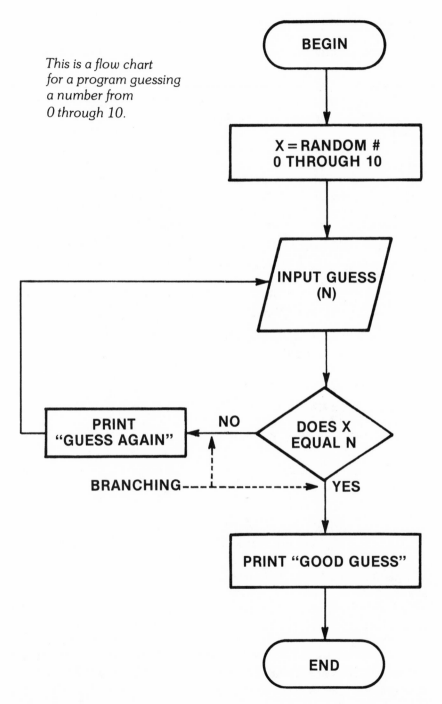

This is a flow chart for a program guessing a number from 0 through 10.

BEGIN

X = RANDOM #
0 THROUGH 10

INPUT GUESS
(N)

PRINT
"GUESS AGAIN"

NO

DOES X
EQUAL N

BRANCHING

YES

PRINT "GOOD GUESS"

END

flow of control (FLOH UV kun•TROHL) *n*. While a program is controlling the operation of a computer, instructions are being executed one after the other. Flow of control means the sequence in which control of the computer passes from one instruction to another. Certain kinds of instructions directly influence the flow of control: for example an instruction which tells the computer which of several instructions to execute next, depending on the status of some indicator.

format (FOR•mat) *n*. The way that information is arranged. For example, the widths of margins on a typed page is part of that page's format. The size allowed to records in a file is part of that file's format. The size of files on a disk is part of that disk's format.

FORTRAN (FOR•tran) *n*. Acronym for FORmula TRANslation. A programming language used widely, mostly for mathematical and scientific tasks.
Here is a sample of a FORTRAN program designed to analyze a True-False questionnaire of 50 questions.

```
        LOGICAL ANS (5Ø)
        READ (5,1ØØ) ANS
        KOUNT = Ø
        DO 1Ø I = 1, 5Ø
        IF (ANS (I) ) KOUNT = KOUNT + 1
    1Ø  CONTINUE
        WRITE (6,2ØØ) KOUNT
        STOP
  1ØØ   FORMAT (5Ø L1)
  2ØØ   FORMAT (1X, I3)
        END
```

frequency (FREE•kwen•see) *n*. Some electrical signals carry impulses that repeat periodically. One use for such a signal is to provide a measurement of time. The number of times such a signal repeats its impulses in a unit of time is called its frequency. Electronic frequencies can be very fast, a million repetitions a second, or more.

function (FUNGK•shun) *n*. Loosely, any single action that a computer can perform. Properly, an action that consists of a single mathematical procedure; for example addition is a function, finding the square root of a number is a function, calculating the differential of an equation is a function.

gap (GAP) *n*. An empty space left between blocks of information on a disk or tape. A gap allows the computer to tell where one block of information ends and another begins.

generation (jen·uh·RAY·shun)*v*., *n*. This term has two meanings. One means the same as production or creation, as in the generation of random numbers; that is a list of random numbers produced by a computer. The other means computers made during the same period of time and using advances not available to earlier computers. For example, the first generation of computers used vacuum tubes, but the second generation used transistors.

graphics (GRAF•iks) *n.* Information displayed in the form of pictures. Computers can display either graphics or text, using different parts of their electronics. The graphics part can display pictures of text characters, however, which are considered graphics.

graphics, low resolution (GRAF•iks LOH rez•uh•LOO•shun) *n.* Computer graphics consist of many dots. If those dots are relatively large, the picture is called low resolution. It will have rougher edges and less detail than if the dots were smaller.

graphics program (GRAF•iks PROH•gram) *n.* A computer program which lets the computer produce graphics.

Here is an ATARI graphics program that prints the word "HI" on your screen.

```
NEW
1Ø GR. 3
2Ø SETCOLOR 4,7,8
3Ø COLOR 1:SETCOLOR Ø,1,8
4Ø PLOT 6,2:DRAWTO 6,17
5Ø PLOT 17,2:DRAWTO 17,17
6Ø PLOT 6,9:DRAWTO 17,9
7Ø PLOT 24,6:DRAWTO 24,17
8Ø PLOT 24,4
9Ø END
```

graphics tablet (GRAF•iks TAB•lit) *n.* A flat device which plugs into a computer. By moving a magnetic pencil over the tablet, a user can draw a picture which will be sent to the computer.

grid (GRID) *n.* A surface that is divided into squares, like graph paper. A computer display may be marked off into a grid, which aids in creating some kinds of graphics.

Hh

hand-held computer (HAND•held kum•PYOO•tur) *n.* A very small computer with a keyboard and usually a one-line display. They are portable, but when away from plug-in devices like a disk drive or a monitor, their usefulness is limited.

handshaking (HAND•shayk•ing) *n.* A jargon term for special timing signals that are exchanged by two electronic devices communicating with each other. For example, if a computer is sending data to a printer, the printer receives some data and tells the printer to stop sending while it prints. When it is done printing it tells the computer to send more data. The signals which tell the computer to start and stop sending are called handshaking signals.

hard copy (HAHRD KOP•ee) *n.* Data from a computer that has been put into some permanent form. A typed page is hard copy. A monitor display or data on erasable tape is not.

hardware (HAHRD•wair) *n.* The parts of a computer system that are electrical or mechanical devices, including circuits, keyboards, chips, printed circuit boards, monitors, etc.

heuristic (hyuu•RIS•tik) *adj.* Solving a problem by exploring it and changing the method of solution as you go; that is, learning while solving. The opposite of algorithmic, which is solving a problem according to a procedure that does not change.

hex (HEKS) *adj.* Abbreviation for hexadecimal.

hexadecimal (hek•sa•DES•i•mul) *adj.* Another word for base sixteen numbering system.

hierarchical (HIGH•uh•rahr•ki•kul) *adj.* Organized in levels, each one including all the ones below it. For example, your body, seen hierarchically, is a single thing at its highest level. At the next level it is two arms, two legs, a trunk, a neck and a head. At the lowest level it is millions and millions of tiny cells. Computer systems are often simpler to think about if they are seen as hierarchies, with each level divided into lower levels. That way you need only think about one level at a time, without being confused by details. For instance you can think about how a computer controls a printer without thinking about how integrated circuits work.

high-level language (HIGH•lev•ul LANG•gwij) *n.* A computer language that is easier for people to understand than low-level language, which is easier for a computer to understand. High-level languages are slower than low-level languages, but much easier to learn.

Here is a sample of high-level language:

```
10 CLS
20 A = 1
30 PRINT A
40 A = A + 1
50 IF A > 10 THEN 70
60 GOTO 30
70 END
```

67

home computer (HOHM kum•PYOO•tur) *n*. A loose term for a microcomputer. Most people who use computers at home use microcomputers, especially the least expensive of the microcomputers. Home computers tend to be used for games, household finances and to receive information from information utilities.

IBM card (EYE BEE EM KAHRD) *n.* A piece of thin cardboard in which holes can be punched in patterns that represent data. Devices can be attached to computers so that they can read the data on these cards. Actually, the idea of punched cards for holding data came long before the first computer.

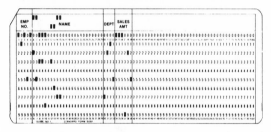

IC (EYE SEE) *n.* Abbreviation for Integrated Circuit.

identifier (eye•DEN•ti•fye•ur) *n*. A word used to identify a memory location; for example, the name of a file in mass storage. When the computer is expecting a file name, and it receives the identifier, it recognizes that word as standing for a number. That number is the location of the start of the file on a disk or tape. Identifiers also stand for memory locations of programs or parts of programs.

illegal operation (i•LEE•gul op•uh•RAY•shun) *n*. An operation which a program instructs the computer to perform, but which the computer cannot perform correctly or at all. For example, if a computer has no graphics capability and you instruct it to draw a shape, it might do nothing, or it might do something meaningless.

image (IM•ij) *n*. This term can mean two things. One is a picture created with an optical instrument, such as a television camera, a film camera or a xerox machine. The other is an exact copy of a section of memory that has been transferred to another section of memory or to a different location in mass storage.

immediate mode (i•MEE•dee•it MOHD) *n*. Giving instructions directly to a computer keyboard or other input device. This is the opposite of deferred mode, in which instructions are recorded, and then played back to the computer, as in a program.

impact printer (IM•pakt PRIN•tur) *n.* Any printer which puts data on paper by striking an inked ribbon. Impact printers may form letters out of dots or with raised faces, like typewriters. They may print one character at a time or a whole line.

increment (ING•kruh•ment) *v.* To increase the value of a number. For example, a program that counts people going though a turnstile would set aside a memory location to hold the number of people. Every time the turnstile turned, the computer would increment that number by one.

index (IN•deks) *n.* Often blocks of data are moved around in memory. Therefore, a datum will not always be at the same location, but it will always be at the same location relative to the beginning of the block. This distance from the beginning of a movable block of data is called an index.

industrial robot (in•DUS•tri•ul ROH•bot) *n.* A machine used to perform tasks in a factory automatically. A robot has its own computer and sensing devices so that it can perform jobs which require adjusting to changing conditions.

information (in•for•MAY•shun) *n.* Data which means something to a person. All information is composed of data, but not all data is information. For example a jumble of letters would be data, but an understandable word is information. Information can also be pictures, code, electrical impulses or any other data that has meaning.

information retrieval (in•for•MAY•shun ri•TREE•vul) *n.* The procedures used to search through a large body of information to find a specific piece of information. Information retrieval depends on being able to catalog information so that you have a way of telling the computer what to look for.

information utility (in•for•MAY•shun yoo•TIL•i•tee) *n*. A company which offers computer data to the average person. A home computer can receive games, financial information, library information and many other kinds of computer services from an information utility over the phone lines.

initialize a disk (i•NISH•ul•ize AY DISK) *v*. A process performed automatically by a computer. It records various signals on the disk which become markers. Afterward, the computer can find a location on the disk by counting these markers.

initialize a variable (i•NISH•ul•ize AY VAIR•ee•uh•bul) *n*. A program stores a variable in a memory location. Whatever number was in that location when a program began will be the variable value until changed. Since that number might be anything, variables are usually set to a starting value, often zero, when a program begins. This is called initializing the variable.

input (IN•puut) *n*. Loosely, any data entering a piece of equipment. Specifically, data received by a CPU from devices connected to it.

input device (IN•puut di•VICE) *n*. A device used to send data to a computer's CPU; for example, a keyboard, a card reader, or a graphics tablet.

One type of input device is a card reader.

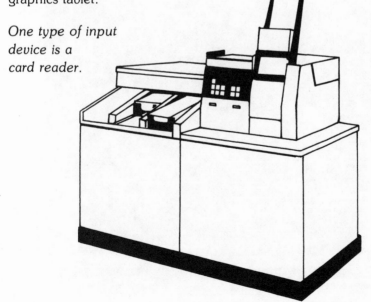

instruction (in•STRUK•shun) *n*. A character or group of characters which represent, in code, an operation for the computer to perform, and the memory locations and values involved in performing it.

instruction set (in•STRUK•shun SET) *n*. Every microprocessor is designed to perform certain operations. Each of these operations is very simple, but they can be repeated and combined into sequences to do very complicated jobs. Together, these simple operations are called the microprocessor's instruction set, and every model of microprocessor has a slightly different instruction set.

integer (IN•tij•ur) *n*. The whole numbers and their opposites. For example, 2, -1, 0, -415, 19 are all integers, 2 1/2, 5.5, -5/3 and 10.9 are not integers.

integrated circuit (IN•tuh•gray•tud SUR•kit) *n*. An electronic circuit, consisting of many transistors, resistors, diodes, etc., produced on a silicon wafer usually about a quarter of an inch (0.56 cm) square. Integrated circuits are often referred to as 'chips'.

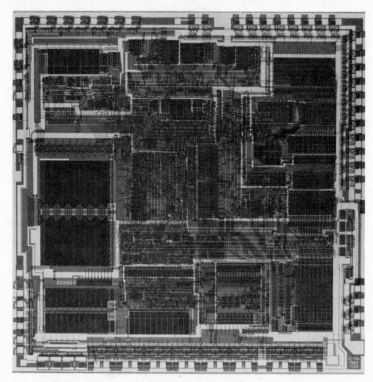

intelligent terminal (in•TEL•i•jent TUR•mi•nul) *n.* A terminal can display data sent to it from a computer to which it is connected. If it can also run its own programs to process that data it is called an intelligent terminal.

interactive (in•tur•AK•tive) *adj.* Letting a person influence the course of a program while it is running. For example, a program which asks the user questions and then acts according to the answer, is interactive. Computers are also used to run video programs which are interactive.

interface (IN•TUR•fays) *n.* Anything that makes it possible for two entities to communicate with each other. Examples are a printed circuit board, which alters data so that it can be transmitted to and from a computer and another device, or a language which a person uses to communicate with a computer.

internal memory (in•TUR•nul MEM•uh•ree) *n.* The memory which is built into a computer, as distinct from mass memory like tapes or disks. A computer can get data from internal memory much more quickly than from mass storage, but mass storage holds much more data.

internal storage (in•TUR•nul STOHR•ij) *n.* The same as internal memory.

interpreter (in•TUR•pri•tur) *n.* A program which translates instructions in a high-level language into machine language. Each instruction is translated into one or more machine language instructions, one at a time.

invalid (in•VAL•id) *adj.* Unacceptable to the computer. For example, a file name that did not exist in a disk directory would be invalid because the computer would not be able to find it.

I/O (EYE•OH) *n.* Abbreviation for Input/Output. It means the part of a computer through which signals pass to and from the CPU and peripheral devices such as printers, disk drives, monitors, keyboards, or remote terminals.

jack (JAK) *n.* A socket into which an electronic connecting wire may be plugged. For example, the hole in a tape recorder where the earphones plug in is an earphone jack.

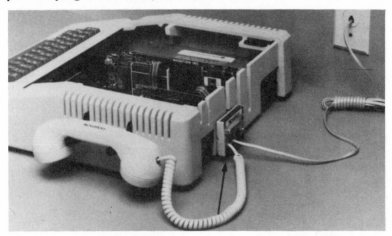

jargon (JAHR•gun) *n.* Words used to describe things by the people who work with those things, but which other people do not understand. For example, computer programmers use the word kludge to mean a hasty, makeshift solution to an error in a program. Few people who are not programmers know what a kludge is.

black box

chip

down time

language

canned program

handshaking

job (JOHB) *n.* The running of several programs to solve a problem or accomplish a result. For example, bringing a company's financial records up to date would be a job. To accomplish it, you might run a payroll program, an accounts receivable program, a general ledger program, and so on.

job control langauge (JOHB kun•TROHL LANG•gwij) *n.* A programming language used in programs which control the procedures needed to run a job on a large computer. These procedures include scheduling, allocating memory space and outside devices needed, charging the job to a department within a company, etc.

joystick (JOI•stik) *n.* A lever mounted on a ball joint within a box so that it can move in any direction. Connected to a computer, a joystick is used to move the cursor on a display monitor. It is usually used with programs that play games or manipulate graphic designs.

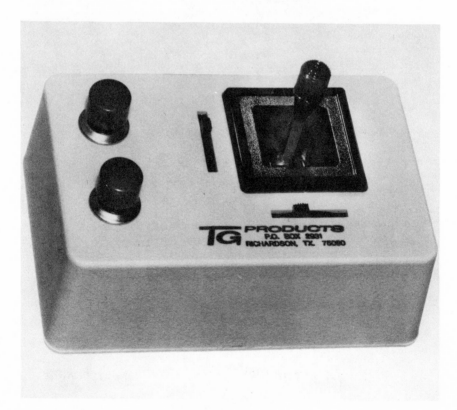

jump (JUMP) *n.* In programming, a jump is when the computer executes an instruction that does not follow the previous instruction sequentially. For example, executing instructions one, two, three and seven would be a jump to instruction seven.

justify (JUS•ti•fye) *v.* To rearrange text so that the first and/or last characters in every line form a straight column down the display or, when printed, down the page.

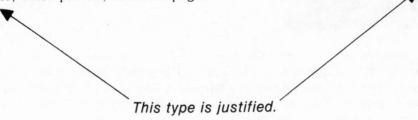

This type is justified.

keyboard (KEE•bohrd) *n*. The rows of keys which you press with your fingers to send signals to a typewriter or computer. In computer keyboards, each key pressed sends an electronic signal that represents a different letter, number or other character.

keypunch (KEE•punch) *n*. A machine with a keyboard that is used to punch holes in cards or tape. Each key pressed automatically punches in a card the holes which represent the character of that key.

key word (KEE WURD) *n*. This term has two meanings. One is a word which is used as an instruction or part of an instruction in a programming langauge. Such a word may not be used for any other purpose in programs written in that language. The other meaning is a word for which a computer searches when retrieving information. For example, files in a data base may hold titles of magazine articles. If the computer is given the key word money it will find all the titles which include that word.

kilo (KEE•loh) *adj*. A prefix which means one thousand. For instance a kilogram means one thousand grams. In computers, however, memory is measured in powers of two, and two to the tenth is 1024. So a kilobyte of memory is not one thousand bytes, but 1024 bytes.

language (LANG•gwij) *n.* Jargon term for programming language.

large scale integration (LARJ SKAYL in•tuh•GRAY•shun) *n.* The process of combining a hundred or more tiny electronic components on a single chip of silicon, as in an integrated circuit.

LCD (EL SEE DEE) *n.* Abbreviation for Liquid Crystal Display. A way of displaying data by using substances that change color when they receive an electrical signal. Some digital watches and hand held computers use LCD displays.

least significant digit (LEEST sig•NIF•i•kunt DIJ•it) *n.* In a number with more than one digit, the digit that stands for the smallest value. For example, in the number 1234, the number four stands for four and is the least significant digit. The number one stands for one thousand and is the most significant digit.

LED (EL EE DEE) *n.* Abbreviation for Light Emitting Diode. An electrical device which converts electricity directly into light. It looks something like a tiny lightbulb.

library (LYE•brer•ee) *n.* A collection of parts of programs. Each part performs a specific task. They can be kept and used as parts of new programs, saving the time of writing them from scratch.

light pen (LITE PEN) *n.* An optical instrument that looks like a ball point pen, but it can detect light. A light pen connected to a computer can be used to draw graphics directly on the monitor screen.

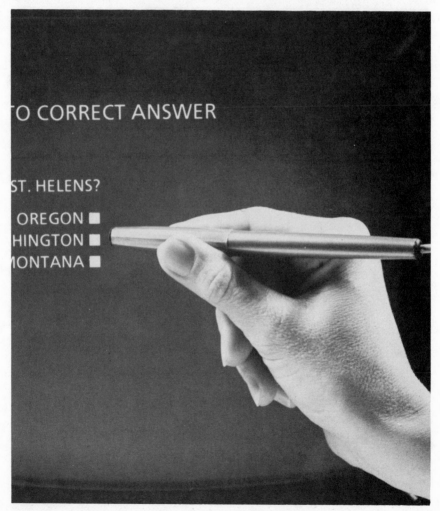

line (LINE) *n.* This term has two meanings. One is a line drawn by a computer as part of a graphic. The other is a line of text on a display or a typed page. A line of text means the space from left to right in which characters could go, even if it is left blank.

line feed (LINE FEED)*n.* The act of advancing to the next line of text. This might be moving the cursor down one line on a monitor display or advancing the paper in a printer so that it types on the next line.

line number (LINE NUM•bur) *n.* Programs written in some programming languages are organized by lines. Each line contains one or more instructions. Each line is given a number, and the computer begins executing the program with the lowest-numbered line.

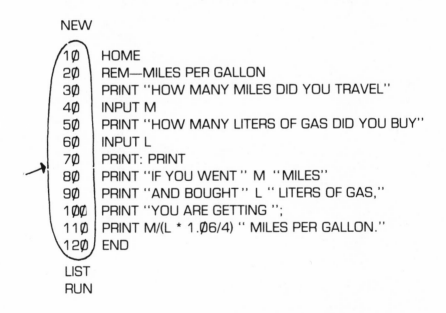

```
NEW

 1Ø    HOME
 2Ø    REM—MILES PER GALLON
 3Ø    PRINT "HOW MANY MILES DID YOU TRAVEL"
 4Ø    INPUT M
 5Ø    PRINT "HOW MANY LITERS OF GAS DID YOU BUY"
 6Ø    INPUT L
 7Ø    PRINT: PRINT
 8Ø    PRINT "IF YOU WENT " M "MILES"
 9Ø    PRINT "AND BOUGHT " L " LITERS OF GAS,"
1ØØ    PRINT "YOU ARE GETTING ";
11Ø    PRINT M/(L * 1.Ø6/4) " MILES PER GALLON."
12Ø    END

LIST
RUN
```

listing (LIST•ing) *n.* A display or print-out of a program.

LOAD (LOHD) *v.* This term has two meanings. One is to transfer data from mass storage into a computer's internal memory. The other is to put a storage medium, like a disk or tape cassette, into the device which can "read" it, like a disk drive or tape player. The second meaning is usually only applied to large systems, not to microcomputers.

logging on (or in) (LAWG·ing ON) *v.* When you first begin to use some computers, especially large computers connected to several terminals besides the one you are using, you must give it certain information. This information might include your name and a password. Giving the computer this information is called logging on, and the computer will not let you use it until you have logged on correctly.

logic (LOJ·ik) *n.* This term has two meanings. One is the part of a computer or circuit which can make decisions, as distinct from the parts which are used for memory. The other is the arrangement of electronic parts in the design of a piece of electronic equipment.

logical operation (LOJ·i·kul op·uh·RAY·shun) *n.* An operation in which a computer makes a decision, as distinct from one in which it performs arithmetic. For example, if a computer does one of two things, depending on whether a condition is true or false, that is a logical operation.

LOGO (LOH·go) *n.* A programming language used primarily in education. LOGO is relatively easy to learn, and is used to teach children the fundamentals of programming. Its distinctive feature is the use of figures called turtles which students can program to move about the display screen, thereby learning the principles of simple geometry. LOGO is one of the few programming languages whose name is not an acronym for anything.

This program, written in TI LOGO, will create a red ball and make it trace a square.

```
TO SQUARE
TELL SPRITE 1
CARRY :BALL
SETCOLOR :RED
HOME
SET SPEED 1Ø
REPEAT 4(WAIT 3Ø RIGHT 9Ø)
SET SPEED Ø
END
```

loop (LOOP) *n.* In a program, you often want the computer to do something over and over again. For example, in a simple program for counting people going through a turnstile, the computer would wait for the turnstile to move, then it would add a number to the total, then it would start over, waiting again. That is called a loop.

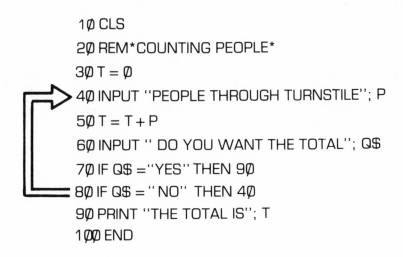

```
10 CLS
20 REM*COUNTING PEOPLE*
30 T = 0
40 INPUT "PEOPLE THROUGH TURNSTILE"; P
50 T = T + P
60 INPUT " DO YOU WANT THE TOTAL"; Q$
70 IF Q$ ="YES" THEN 90
80 IF Q$ = " NO" THEN 40
90 PRINT "THE TOTAL IS"; T
100 END
```

LSI (EL ES EYE) *n.* Abbreviation for Large Scale Integration.

machine language (muh•SHEEN LANG•gwij) *n.* A programming language in which all instructions are coded as binary numbers, so that any number or letter is expressed as a combination of ones and zeros. Before a computer can run a program it must be translated into machine language, usually by a translator program such as an assembler or a compiler.

Here is an eight-step program written in machine code and arranged in hex format.

Step Number	Machine Code	Explanation
0	1011 1000	Load decimal 32 in
1	0010 0000	register RO
2	1011 1010	Load decimal 5 in
3	0000 0101	register R2
4	0000 1001	Load port 1 to accumulator
5	1111 0000	Transfer contents of accumulator to register addressed by register 0
6	0001 1000	Increment RO by 1
7	1110 1010	Decrement register 2 by 1: if result
8	0000 0100	is zero, continue to step 9; if not go to step 4
9		
10		

machine readable (muh•SHEEN REE•duh•bul) *n.* Data which is in some form that can be "read" by an input device and sent to a computer. For example, punched cards are machine readable and so are the special numbers printed on the bottom of cashed bank checks.

magnetic core (mag•NET•ik KOHR) *n.* A small ring made partly of iron. Such a ring can be magnetized by an electric current. Magnetic cores are used as internal memory units in very large computers.

magnetic disk (mag•NET•ik DISK) *n*. The same as a disk; used for mass memory storage.

magnetic drum (mag•NET•ik DRUM) *n*. A cylinder coated with a kind of magnetic material like that used on disks or tapes. Drums are used for mass memory storage.

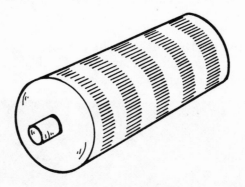

magnetic ink character recognition (mag•NET•ik INGK KAIR•ik•tur rek•ug•NISH•un) *n*. The ability of computers to read messages written in special magnetic ink. This ink contains tiny particles of iron. If a character is printed with magnetic ink, special input devices can tell which character it is. The specially shaped numbers on the bottoms of bank checks are printed in magnetic ink.

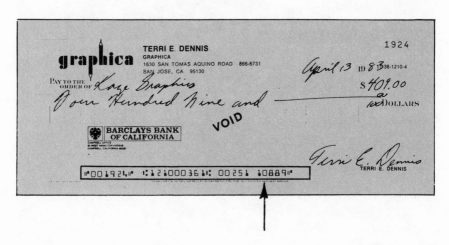

magnetic media (mag•NET•ik MEE•dee•uh) *n.* Any material with which data can be recorded magnetically, including tape, disks, drums, or magnetic ink.

magnetic tape (mag•NET•ik TAYP) *n.* Tape made of thin plastic coated with iron oxide, exactly like the tape used to record music. It is also used to record data sent to it by a computer. That data can then be sent back to the computer.

main frame (MAYN FRAYM) *adj.* The largest kind of computer is referred to as a main frame because the CPU of such a machine used to be mounted on a characteristic frame.

main memory (MAYN MEM•uh•ree) *n.* Another term for internal memory; the memory within a computer, as distinct from memory stored on tapes, disks, or other mass storage.

main storage (MAYN STOR•ij) *n.* Another term for internal memory.

mantissa (man•TIS•uh) *n.* With computers, mantissa usually means that part of a number to the right of and including the decimal point. For example, in the number 45.567, the mantissa is .567. In mathematics, the term has a slightly different meaning.

MARK I (MARK WUN) *n.* An early computer built at IBM and put into use at Harvard University in 1944. It was more like a mechanical adding-machine than an electronic computer.

mass storage (MAS STOHR•ij) *n.* The recording of data from a computer's internal memory on some medium outside of the computer, such as disks or tapes. Mass storage can hold much more data than internal memory, but it takes much longer for the computer to get data from mass storage.

matrix (MAY•triks) *n.* A way of arranging things into a pattern of horizontal rows and vertical columns. This kind of arrangement has a number of special uses, among which are converting data from one code to another, and performing certain kinds of mathematical tasks.

A,0	A,1	A,2	A,3
B,0	B,1	B,2	B,3
C,0	C,1	C,2	C,3
D,0	D,1	D,2	D,3
E,0	E,1	E,2	E,3

medium (MEE•dee•um) *n.* A vehicle for carrying information. For example, a newspaper is a medium of printed information and a television is a medium of electronic information. In the computer world, media include magnetic disks and tapes.

memory (MEM•uh•ree) *n.* The part of a computer system which holds data. Memory can be inside the computer, for example, in special chips or in magnetic cores or it can be outside the computer, in mass storage such as disks.

memory address (MEM•uh•ree AD•res) *n*. A location within a computer's memory. Each such location is given a number, called its address. Thus, memory addresses are simply numbers used to locate data within memory.

memory capacity (MEM•uh•ree kuh•PAS•i•tee) *n*. The amount of data a computer's memory can hold. Memory is measured in kilo-bytes; that is, blocks of one thousand and twenty-four bytes. For instance, a home computer may have a memory of 48K, or 48 kilo-bytes.

memory map (MEM•uh•ree MAP) *n*. Different sections of a computer's memory are used for different purposes: one section may store programs, another variables, another the operating system, and so on. A memory map is simply a diagram which shows which sections of memory are used for which purpose.

menu (MEN•yoo) *n.* A list of actions which a computer can take, displayed on a monitor. Many interactive programs use menus to show the user what instructions he may give the computer, and he can simply select the one he wants from the menu.

menu driven (MEN•yoo DRIV•en) *adj.* A program which uses a lot of menus. With such a program, all or most of the instructions a user gives to the computer he selects from one or more menus.

microcomputer (MY•kroh•kum•PYOO•tur) *n.* The smallest kind of computer. Originally microcomputers were those whose CPUs were all on one chip, called a microprocessor. Now, larger computers also use microprocessors, and in fact the line between microcomputers and minicomputers is becoming very blurred.

microdisk (MY•kroh•disk) *n.* A floppy disk that is just over three inches (7.62 cm) in diameter.

microprocessor (MY·kroh·PROS·es·ur) *n.* An entire central processing unit, the part of a computer that makes it work, produced in the form of an integrated circuit.

microsecond (MY·kroh SEK·und) *n.* One millionth of a second.

minicomputer (MIN·ee·kum·PYOO·tur) *n.* The middle-size computer, smaller than a mainframe and larger than a microcomputer. Originally minicomputers were much cheaper than mainframes, and they were faster and could do more than microcomputers. Today, it is hard to tell the difference between large minis and small mainframes and between small minis and large micros.

minidisk (MIN·ee·disk) *n.* A floppy disk that is five and one-quarter inches (13.34 cm) in diameter.

misfeed (MIS·feed) *n.* When paper, punched cards, or some other medium does not move through a device as it is supposed to. For example, if a punched card is folded, it might jam up a card reader, causing a misfeed.

mnemonic (ni•MON•ik) *n.* A word that is easy to remember. For instance, a coded instruction for the computer to add two numbers might be 10000110 in machine language, which is hard to remember. The same instruction in assembly language might be ADD, which is a mnemonic.

mode (MOHD) *n.* A category of operation. For example, a computer drawing graphics is said to be in the graphics mode.

MODEM (MOH•dum) *n.* Acronym for MOdulator-DEModulator. A device which changes data from a computer into a form which can be transmitted over phone lines or other long-distance carriers.

module (MOJ•ool) *n.* A building block that is part of a larger item. For example, in a computer system, the CPU, the monitor, the disk drive might all be modules. Programs are also organized into modules, so that one module of the program controls input, another controls display, and so on.

monitor (MON•i•tur) *n.* A device which lets you examine something. Usually the term means a cathode ray tube display, but it also may be a special program which lets you see the contents of the computer's memory and registers or some electronic device which lets you see some other parts of the computer's operation.

MOS (MOS) *n.* Acronym for Metal Oxide Semiconductor. A common kind of integrated circuit made in part from metal oxide and silicon.

most significant digit (MOHST sig•NIF•i•kunt DIJ•it) *n.* In a number with more than one digit, the digit that stands for the largest value. For example, in the number 1234, the number one stands for one thousand and is the most significant digit. The number four stands for four and is the least significant digit.

mouse (MOWS) *n.* A device that is attached to a computer by a long cable and which is rolled along a flat surface by hand. As it rolls, it controls the movement of a cursor on the computer's display. A mouse controls the cursor's direction and speed. Usually, a mouse also has a button or buttons for selecting menu items from the display or for giving commands to the computer.

multiprocessing (MUL•tee•PROS•es•ing) *n.* This can mean a number of things: using more than one computer to perform different tasks in a single job, designing a computer in which processing functions are performed by more than one device, or processing more than one job at the same time on a single computer.

nanosecond (NAN•oh•sek•und) *n.* A billionth of a second.

network (NET•wurk) *n.* As a general term this means a system whose parts are some distance from each other but are connected in some way. A computer network is simply two or more computers and their peripheral devices, all of which can send and receive data from each other.

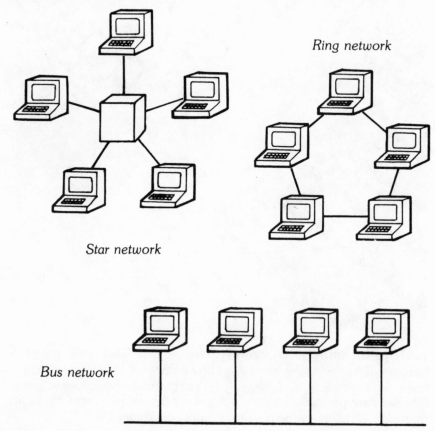

Ring network

Star network

Bus network

nibble (NIBL) *n.* Half of a byte, usually four bits.

non-destructive (non•di•STRUK•tiv) *adj.* This term refers to a cursor which can move over text characters on a display without erasing them.

non-volatile memory (non•VOL•uh•til MEM•uh•ree) *n.* A kind of computer memory which keeps the data stored in it even if the power to the computer is turned off.

number sign (NUM•bur SINE) *n.* Every number is either larger or smaller than zero. Numbers that are smaller than zero are called negative numbers and are always written with a "minus" sign which looks like this: − . Numbers larger than zero are called positive and may be identified with a "plus" sign which looks like this: + . Usually positive numbers are written with no sign.

numeration system (noo•muh•RAY•shun SIS•tum) *n.* Another term for numbering system. A numeration system is a way of expressing the values of numbers; for example, binary, decimal and hex are all numeration systems.

nybble (NIBL) *n.* Another way of spelling nibble.

object program (OB•jikt PROH•gram) *n.* The machine language version of a program after it has been assembled or compiled.

octal (OK•tul) *n.* A base eight numbering system which uses only the digits 0 through 7.

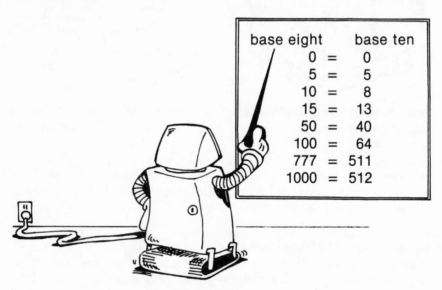

base eight		base ten
0	=	0
5	=	5
10	=	8
15	=	13
50	=	40
100	=	64
777	=	511
1000	=	512

off-line (AWF•line) *adj.* When a job is being performed by a device not under control of a central processing unit. This may mean two things. One is that data is being sent between the computer and some device to which it is not connected. For example, data might be recorded on tape "off-line" and then carried by hand to the computer's tape player. The other meaning is that a device connected to the computer is operating independently; for example, a printer might be printing a document while the central processor is working on something completely different.

on-line (AWN•line) *adj.* When a job is being performed by a device under control of a central processing unit. For example, if a printer is printing data as it is received from the CPU, according to timing signals received from the CPU, the printer is said to be "on-line".

op code (OP KOHD) *n.* Abbreviation for Operation Code.

operand (OP•uh•rand) *n.* The object of an operation. For example, the operation code MOV n,l might mean move the number represented by n to the memory location represented by l. Here, n and l are operands. (MOV is the operator.)

operating system (OP•uh•rayt•ing SIS•tum) *n.* A special program or group of programs which controls all the activities of a computer system. For example, an operating system might control the transfer of data to and from peripheral devices, might determine where to put programs and other data in memory, might protect data through the use of user passwords, might keep track of how much time each user spends on the system, and so on.

operation (op•uh•RAY•shun) *n.* An elementary action that a computer can take, such as adding two numbers or moving a number from one location to another.

operation code (op•uh•RAY•shun KOHD) *n*. A code symbol for an operator. For example, the operation code MOV n, l might mean move the number represented by n to the memory location represented by l . Here, n and l are operands. (MOV is the operator.)

optical character recognition (OP•ti•kul KAIR•ik•tur rek•ug•NISH•un) *n*. A method by which computers can read numbers and letters written on paper. Usually these numbers and letters have to have special shapes, like the numbers on the bottom of cancelled checks. Optical character recognition consists of an optical scanning system and a recognition system.

optical scanner (OP•ti•kul SKAN•nur) *n*. A device which can tell whether a mark is present on a piece of paper by measuring the amount of light reflected from the paper. Each number and letter is made of marks in different positions. An optical scanner can tell which marks are in which positions. Another device called a recognition system can tell which letter the scanner is looking at, depending on the arrangement of the marks.

output (OWT•puut) *n*. Any data sent from a device. For example, data may be sent from a computer to a printer, which would then type the data. Leaving the computer the data would be output. Entering the printer it would be input.

output device (OWT•puut di•VICE) *n.* Any device which produces stored data out of the electronic data processed inside a computer. For example, a disk drive produces data on a magnetic disk; a printer produces data typed on paper.

overflow (oh•vur•FLOH) *n.* When a computer operation produces too much data to fit in the amount of memory set aside for it. For example, if the result of an addition problem was too large to fit in its assigned memory location or if a block of text became too large to fit in its assigned file.

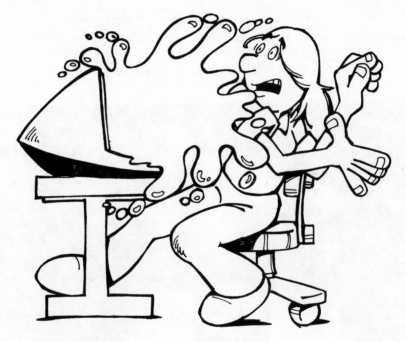

overwrite (oh•vur•RITE) *v.* To put data in a part of memory or of a magnetic medium where other data had been, thereby erasing that other data.

paddle (PADL) *n.* A device, usually held in the hand, which is connected to a computer. By turning a dial on the paddle you can make the cursor move either up and down or right and left. Paddles are used on home computers, mostly to play games.

paper tape (PAY•pur TAYP) *n.* A strip of tape in which are punched rows of holes. The pattern of holes in each row is a code for a character. Paper tape can be used to store data from a computer and to enter that data back into a computer.

paper tape reader (PAY•pur TAYP REE•dur) *n.* A device through which paper tape is fed. It converts the patterns of holes in the tape into electronic signals. These signals are sent to a computer.

parallel (PAIR•uh•lel) *adj.* Working or traveling side by side. For example, a byte of data consists of eight bits. If the data is transmitted in parallel, every byte sent goes out as eight bits, each on a different wire, all at the same time. If the transmission were serial instead of parallel, each bit would go out at a different time, one after the other, on the same wire.

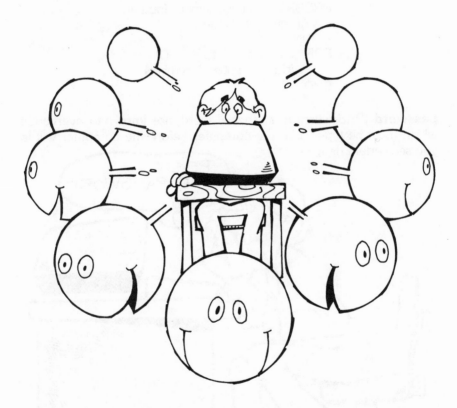

parameter (puh•RAM•i•tur) *n.* Some commands or parts of programs carry out actions which vary according to the value of some number or letter. These numbers are called parameters. For example, take a program selected from a block of text all the words that start with a given letter. The letter given to that program would be its parameter. The term is used interchangeably with the term argument.

parenthesis (puh•REN•thuh•sis) *n.* Either of the two characters which look like this: ( ). In a program a parenthesis may have a special meaning.

PASCAL (pas•KAL) *n.* One of the most popular programming languages. It is named after the seventeenth century French mathematician, Blaise Pascal.

A PASCAL program that instructs the computer to print the squares of the numbers from 1 to 10 would look like this:

```
PROGRAM SquareNumber (output);
   VAR number:integer;
BEGIN
FOR number : = 1 to 10 DO
      Writeln (number * number);
END.
```

password (PAS•wurd) *n.* A special word, not known to everybody, which must be typed into the computer before the computer will let you see certain data.

PEEK (PEEK) *n.* To display the contents of a single memory location.

percent sign (pur•SENT SINE) *n.* The character that looks like this: %. In a computer program it may have a special meaning.

period (PEER•ee•ud) *n.* The character that looks like this: .. In a computer program it may have a special meaning.

peripheral (puh•RIF•uh•ruhl) *n.* A device external to the CPU and memory of a computer. For example, disk drives, printers, light pens, keyboards and CRT displays.

personal computer (PUR•suh•nul kum•PYOO•tur) *n.* Any microcomputer which is small enough that many individuals can afford it. These computers are for home, hobby and professional use. They have made computers available to large numbers of people for the first time.

picosecond (PEE•koh•sek•und) *n.* A trillionth of a second.

PIXEL (PIKSL) *n.* An acronym for PICture ELement. A display on a CRT monitor or television screen is composed of thousands of tiny dots. These dots are called pixels.

plotter (PLAWT•ur) *n.* A device connected to a computer and used to draw pictures or diagrams.

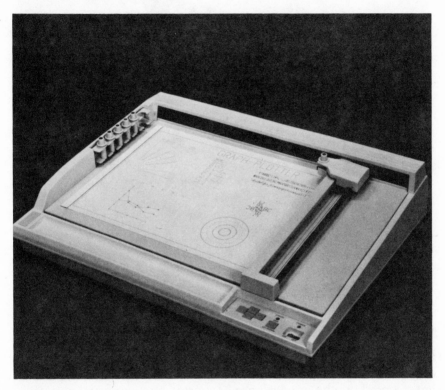

plus sign (PLUS SINE) *n.* The character which looks like this: +. In a program, the plus sign may have a special meaning.

POKE (POHK) *v.* To enter a value into a single memory location.

port (POHRT) *n.* A destination to which the computer sends data or from which it receives data. Ports are given addresses as are memory locations. For example, data going to a printer from a CPU would be sent to an output port. The term refers not to the physical connection between computer and printer, but to the address which indicates where the information should be sent.

pound sign (POWND SINE) *n*. The character that looks like this: £. In a program, the pound sign may have a special meaning.

print out (PRINT OWT) *n*. Data from a computer that has been printed on paper by some device connected to the computer.

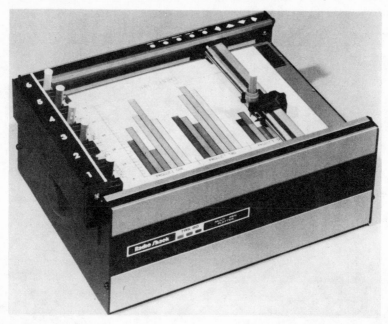

printed circuit (PRIN•tud SUR•kit) *n*. An electronic circuit consists of resistors, capacitors, diodes and many other components connected together in various arrangements. In a printed circuit, the connections are strips of metal printed onto a flat piece of plastic. The components are soldered into holes which are connected by these printed strips.

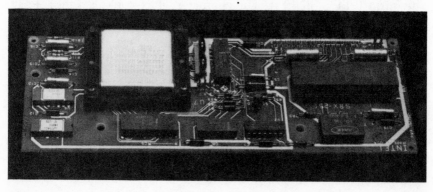

printer (PRINT•ur) *n.* A device mainly used to convert data in a computer into characters printed on paper. Some printers can also be used to print graphics.

priority (pry•OR•i•tee) *n.* In a chain of tasks to be done one after the other, the place of a given task. For example, the task to be done first has the highest priority.

processing (PROS•es•ing) *n.* A very broad term that means any manipulation of data. Data may be rearranged, changed, encoded, decoded, addressed to memory or to a peripheral device or manipulated in some other way. Processing is what happens to data between the time that it enters and leaves a computer's CPU.

program (PROH•gram) *n.* A list of instructions for a computer to follow. A program is written in a programming language and can be stored in the computer's memory. The original version of the program, written by a programmer, is called source code and may be written on paper, punched on paper cards or tape, and entered directly into the computer's memory. In any case, it must be in the computer's memory before it can be run on that computer.

programmer (PROH•gram•ur) *n.* A person who composes a computer program.

programming language (PROH•gram•ing LANG•gwij) *n.* One of many codes in which programs are written by programmers. The lowest level of programming languages is machine language, which consists of only ones and zeros. Assembly language is the next higher level. Most programming languages are high-level such as BASIC, PASCAL, FORTRAN or COBOL.

PROM (PROM) *n.* Acronym for Programmable Read Only Memory. One or more chips of ROM into which data may be entered by using a special device. Generally, once data is entered into PROM, it cannot be changed; that is, it becomes ROM.

prompt (PROMPT) *n.* A character or mark that appears on a CRT display indicating that the computer is waiting for the user to enter data. Some common prompts are: an asterisk, a question mark, the word 'ready?' and an arrowhead (>).

punch card (PUNCH KARD) *n.* The same as an IBM card.

Qq

question mark (KWES•chun MARK) *n.* The character that looks like this: ?. In a program a question mark might have a special meaning.

queue (KYOO) *n.* A chain of tasks waiting to be processed by a computer. Tasks in queue are assigned priorities and await their turn to be given the computer's attention.

quote mark (KWOHT MARK) *n.* A character that looks like this: ". In a program quote marks may have a special meaning.

QWERTY (KWER•tee) *adj.* The traditional layout of keys on a keyboard. The six alphabetical keys on the upper left of the keyboard spell out QWERTY.

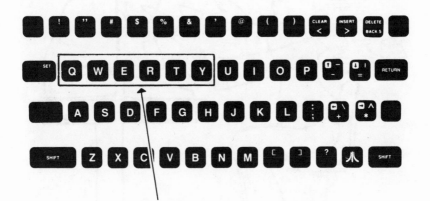

RAM (RAM) *n.* Acronym for Random Access Memory. Data can be put into RAM, stored there and taken out again for processing. The computer can get data from any location in RAM as fast as from any other. RAM makes up most of the internal memory of a computer.

RAM card (RAM KARD) *n.* A printed circuit board containing RAM chips. By plugging such a board into some computers, their internal memory can be increased.

random (RAN•dum) *adj.* An arrangement of things in which no one thing has any precedence over any other. For example, a random selection of numbers is a group of numbers in which no number is more likely to occur than any other.

random access (RAN•dum AK•ses) *n.* The ability to put data into or take it out of any location with as much ease as any other. This applies to storage locations as well as internal memory locations.

read (REED) *v.* When a device gets data from another device, we say that it is reading that data. For example, a computer reads data from a disk.

real number (REEL NUM•bur) *n.* Almost all numbers are called real numbers: positive numbers, negative numbers, zero, decimal numbers are all real. Mathematicians also use imaginary numbers and complex numbers which are not real numbers, but these will not ordinarily be encountered by a computer user.

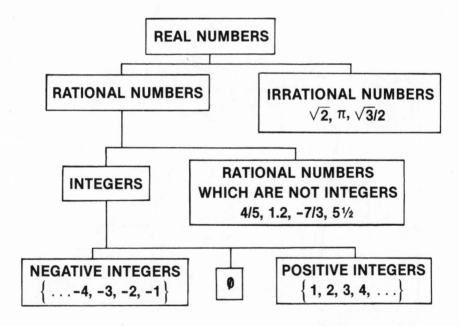

recognition system (rek•ug•NISH•un SIS•tum) *n.* A device which receives data from an optical scanner and translates it into different data. The data coming from an optical scanner represents the marks out of which written letters are made. For example, the letter H is made of two up-down marks and a cross mark in the middle. If a recognition system received the indications that those marks were present, it would send out electrical code for the letter H.

record (REK•urd) *n.* The in-between unit of information storage. A file is divided into records and a record is divided into fields. For example, a data base about life on Earth may contain one file on animals with four legs. This file may include a record on giraffes, a record on horses, a record on crocodiles and so on. The record of each of these animals may include fields on height, weight, habitat or kind of food.

register (REJ•i•stur) *n.* A small amount of memory contained in a CPU. Most CPUs contain several registers. Data to be processed must first be put into one of the registers, usually very briefly. Registers are separate from internal memory.

relative address (REL•uh•tiv AD•res) *n*. A computer's memory is divided into thousands of locations, called memory addresses. A program or other block of data may be placed in that memory starting at a certain address. A single piece of data will have an address within the block, for example, thirty addresses from the beginning of the block. It will have a different address within memory as a whole, for example, thirty thousand addresses from the beginning of memory. The former is its relative address.

reset (REE•set) *v*. To change the number held in a memory location, variable, flag or other value from one to zero.

reset key (REE•set KEE) *n*. A key on a computer keyboard which normally is used to reset the parts of the CPU to the way they were before a program or operation began. This stops a program and might lose any data which the program had put into internal memory. Some programs disable the reset key so that it does nothing, or does something other than stop the program.

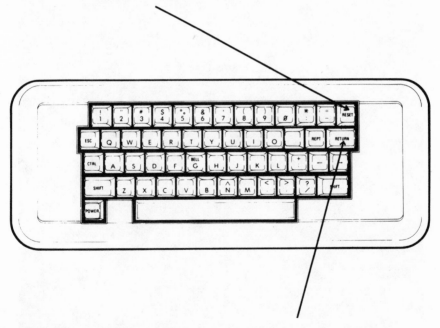

return (ri•TURN) *n*. Another name for the carriage return key.

return key (ri•TURN KEE) *n*. The same as carriage return key.

robot (ROH•bot) *n.* A machine which can perform physical tasks under the control of a computer. Robots are used to weld automobile bodies, to run lathes and to do other manufacturing jobs. These kinds of robots consist of large, mechanical arms which have vise-like graspers at the end, and which can turn in many different directions. Since they are controlled by a computer, they can do any task for which a computer program exists.

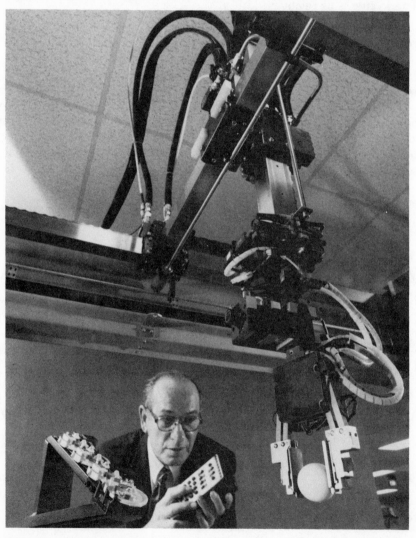

robotics (roh•BOT•iks) *n.* The study and manufacture of robots.

ROM (ROM) *n.* Acronym for Read Only Memory. This kind of memory holds data permanently. It makes up a small part of a computer's internal memory, holding information that controls certain vital operations. The user cannot change this information or put new information into ROM.

routine (roo•TEEN) *n.* A piece of a program. A routine contains the instructions for making the computer perform a single task, and a routine may be used in many different programs. For example, many programs require the user to enter data while the program is running. One routine may let the user enter data, and would be called an input routine. One input routine might be used in many programs.

row (ROH) *n.* When you work with computers, it is often convenient to reduce a large field of information into smaller units. This is done by dividing the large field into horizontal strips called rows and vertical strips called columns. Examples are two-dimensional arrays and monitor screens. Once divided into strips, the crossing strips form boxes, as on a checker board. Each box can then be identified by the number of its row and its column.

RUN (RUN) *v.* To execute a program. In other words, when a computer is performing some job under the control of a program, we say that it is running that program.

SAVE (SAVE) *v.* To transfer data from the computer's internal memory to mass storage. For example, a file is saved to a disk.

scientific notation (sye•un•TIF•ik noh•TAY•shun) *n.* A way of writing numbers, especially very large or very small numbers, as a number between one and ten times a power of ten. For example, in scientific notation 3,560,000,000,000 would be 3.56 × 10 to the 12th; and .000000034 would be 3.4 × 10 to the −8.

scratchpad (SKRACH•pad) *n.* A relatively small amount of internal memory set aside for temporary storage of data. For instance, a program might make all input data go to a scratch pad. Once there, data could be processed in any number of ways depending on what kind of data it is.

screen (SKREEN) *n.* The face of a CRT, where data is displayed.

scroll (SKROHL) *v.* To move across the face of a display. For example, most computers display only about twenty-five lines of text on a monitor at one time. This text must be moved up or down to see the text preceding or following it. When displayed data is moved in this way it is said to scroll.

search (SURCH) *v.* Computers can search through a large block of data and find a given datum. For example, a computer could search through the text of this dictionary and find every occurence of the word 'computer'. It could display each page on which the word was found, or display the numbers of all those pages.

secondary storage (SEK• un•der•ee STOR•ij) *n.* Another word for mass storage.

sector (SEK•tur) *n.* A disk is divided into tracks which are in turn divided into sectors. Tracks are concentric circles on the disk, and each track is divided into a number of sectors. A file may be recorded in more than one sector in more than one track.

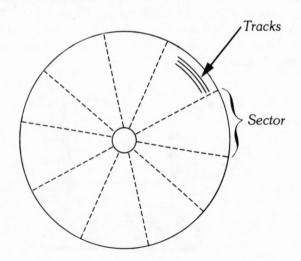

semiconductor (sem•ee•kun•DUK•tur) *n.* A material, such as silicon, that sometimes conducts electricity well, and sometimes not well, depending on certain conditions, such as temperature. Semiconductors are used in transistors and integrated circuits.

semiconductor memory (sem•ee•kun•DUK•tur MEM•uh•ree) *n.* Internal memory in which data is stored in a semiconductor circuit. Certain kinds of semiconductor circuits can maintain a continuous output, either of a high or a low voltage, until signalled to switch to the opposite output. Thus, such memory units can store binary data, in which ones are represented by high voltages and zeros are represented by low voltages.

serial (SEER•ee•ul) *adj.* Working or traveling one after the other. For example, a byte of data consists of eight bits. If the transmission were serial each bit would go out at a different time, one after the other, on the same wire. If the data were transmitted in parallel, each bit would go out on a different wire, all at the same time.

service bureau (SUR•vis BYOOR•oh) *n.* A company that does jobs which require computers for clients who do not want to operate computers themselves. For instance, an accounting service bureau would use its own computers to do computerized bookkeeping and financial reports. Its customers would have to supply only the original figures.

set (SET) *v.* To change the number held in a memory location, variable, flag or other value from zero to one.

shift key (SHIFT KEE) *n.* The key on a keyboard which, when pressed, makes letters print as capitals instead of lower case letters. Sometimes the shift key does not apply to all keys on a computer keyboard.

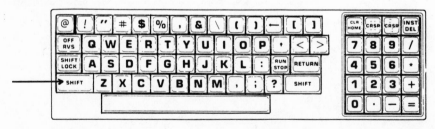

silicon (SIL•i•kon) *n.* An element that is similar to the metals. After oxygen it is the most common element in the earth's crust. It is the main ingredient of semiconductors and therefore makes integrated circuits possible.

Silicon Valley (SIL•i•kon VAL•ee) *n.* An area whose center is about forty miles south of San Francisco. It has a very high concentration of electronics companies including IBM, Intel, Hewlett-Packard, Atari, Apple, Lockheed Missiles and Space, NASA's Ames Research Center, and many others. It is also near Stanford University, which conducts electronics and computer research.

simulation (SIM•yoo•lay•shun) *n.* When a computer produces the results of a procedure so that the procedure does not have to take place. For example, if a computer is given all the information about the design of a new airplane, it can calculate what would happen if that airplane were flown under a number of conditions. That would be a simulation of the airplane's flight.

slash (SLASH) *n.* The character that looks like this: / . In a program, this character may have some special meaning.

software (SAWFT•wair) *n.* A computer system consists of two parts. One is the hardware, that is the physical electronic and mechanical equipment which does things, such as printed circuit boards, disk drives, and keyboards. The other part is the software, that is any kind of program, instructions or other data which tells the hardware what to do.

software library (SAWFT•wair LYE•brer•ee) *n.* A collection of programs and parts of programs which can be used at any time or combined in various ways to produce new programs.

solid-state (SOLD•id-STAYT) *n.* Electronics that use semiconductor circuits such as transistors or integrated circuits instead of vacuum tubes. In a wider sense, this term means any control of electrons within any solid material, as distinct from a gas-filled or vacuum tube. In this sense transformers and core memories are also solid-state devices.

sort (SORT) *v.* To rearrange a block of data into a given order. For example, alphabetizing a group of words would be one way that a computer might sort data. Another way would be to arrange a list of addresses in order of their zip code or of the last name of the addressee.

source code (SOHRS KOHD) *n.* The code in which a program is written originally. The computer automatically translates source code into object code. Object code is machine language which the computer can run.

source program (SOHRS PROH•gram) *n.* A program is originally written in a programming language. Then it is translated by the computer into machine language (ones and zeros that the computer can run). The program as written originally is the source program and the machine language version is the object program.

space bar (SPAYS BAHR) *n.* The long, unmarked key nearest the user on a keyboard. It does not produce any character when pressed, but it does produce an electronic code which stands for one empty space and which is stored in memory just like that of any character.

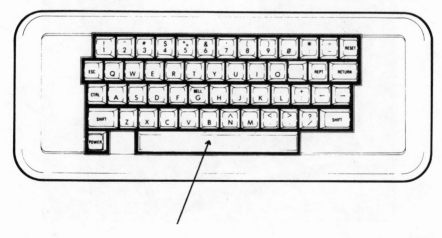

speech, digital (SPEECH, DIJ•i•tul) *n.* Speech can be transformed into digital information for transmission along with computer information or for storage in computer memory. Digital speech, like any digital recording of sound, breaks the sound into tiny units. For example, a word which takes a half second to pronounce might be divided into thousands of units, each one a tiny part of a second in duration. Each of these units has characteristics such as loudness, pitch and so on that can be represented by numbers. These numbers then become a digital code for the speech.

speech synthesis (SPEECH SIN•thuh•sis) *n.* Any sound, including speech, can be represented by a numerical code that can be stored in computer memory. Special devices can convert such a code into recognizable sounds that can be played over loudspeakers. Speech synthesis is production of speech from code.

speech synthesizer (SPEECH sin•thuh•SIZE•ur) *n.* A device which converts numerical code into recognizable speech, usually played over a loudspeaker.

statement (STAYT•ment) *n.* A source program consists of statements. Each statement consists of one or more instructions that tell the computer to perform various operations.

statement number (STAYT•ment NUM•bur) *n.* In some programming languages, including BASIC, each statement is given a number, called its statement number. The computer runs a program written in such a language by executing the lowest numbered statement first.

static RAM (STAT•ik RAM) *n.* Internal memory that does not lose its contents as long as power to the computer is on. Once the computer puts a value into a static memory location, it remains there. The opposite of dynamic RAM.

storage (STOR•ij) *n.* Another word for memory.

storage capacity (STOR•ij kuh•PAS•i•tee) *n.* The amount of data that can be stored in a computer memory. Usually storage capacity is measured in thousands of bytes.

storage device (STOR•ij di•VICE) *n.* A memory device. This term is used loosely to apply to peripheral storage, like disk drives.

It is also used to mean internal computer memory or, specifically, the tiny electronic components which each store a single bit within computer memory.

storage location (STOR•ij loh•KAY•shun) *n.* A position within memory at which a given datum is stored. Storage locations are distinguished among each other by addresses. Each storage location is assigned a memory address, that is, a number of its own.

string (STRING) *n.* A group of characters which the computer treats as a single whole. For example, a word of text consists of several characters. The computer would store the characters of a word in consecutive memory locations. To the computer, that word is a string of characters. A string may also consist of numbers. Numbers in a string are treated as text and cannot be used in arithmetic calculations.

string value (STRING VAL•yoo) *n.* A string of numbers is treated as text and cannot be used in arithmetic calculations. However, a string of numbers can be converted into the same number for calculations, and that number is called the string value. For example, the string "1234" has the string value of 1,234. A string consisting of numbers and letters has the string value of the numbers before the first letter. The string "1234abc567" also has the string value 1,234.

string variable (STRING VAIR •ee•uh•bul) *n.* Some computer languages, notably BASIC, let you use a character to stand for a string. For example, in BASIC, the instruction ST$ = "this is a string" means that whenever the computer sees the symbol ST$, it acts as though it were the string "this is a string". A symbol like ST$ that stands for a string is called a string variable.

Some samples of string variables

```
A$ = "SAM"
Q$ = "YZKMPF"
CITY$ = "SAN FRANCISCO"
MONEY$ = "FIVE HUNDRED DOLLARS"
VALUE$ = "$4.95"
ST$ = "THIS IS A STRING"
```

structured programming (STRUK•churd PROH•gram•ing) *n*. Since people began writing computer programs they have tried to discover methods of writing them in an organized manner so that it would be easier to keep track of the many parts of a program and to tell what a program does by looking at its code. Structured programming includes many methods, but the central ideas are that a program should be divisible into parts and sub-parts, and that each part and sub-part should be executed as the result of only one other part or sub-part.

subroutine (SUB•roo•teen) *n*. A part of a computer program which performs a specific task and is repeated more than once in the course of a program.

```
10 HOME
20 PRINT "I AM"
30 GOSUB 100
40 PRINT "GOING"
50 GOSUB 100
60 PRINT "VERY"
70 GOSUB 100
80 PRINT "SLOW"
90 STOP
100 FOR T = 1 TO 1000
→ 110 NEXT T
120 RETURN
```

supercomputer (SOO•pur•kum•PYOO•tur) *n*. A loose term for the computers at any given time which are faster, more expensive and have more memory than any other computers then in existence.

synchronous (SING•kruh•nus) *adj.* When the operations of a device are timed by a clock. For example, computers contain oscillators, electronic components which emit regular pulses millions of times a second. (Oscillators used in computers are sometimes referred to as clocks.) A synchronous device might begin each of its operations on every fifth pulse. The opposite of asynchronous, in which each operation's conclusion is a signal for the next operation to begin.

syntax (SIN•taks) *n.* The rules for arranging the parts of a statement in any language. In programming languages, each statement must be written in the correct syntax or the computer will not be able to use it. For example, the BASIC instruction to print the word 'alphabet' is: PRINT "ALPHABET". Syntax requires that the quotation marks be present and that PRINT be spelled correctly. Otherwise, the computer will not obey the command.

syntax error (SIN•taks AIR•ur) *n.* What happens when a computer is given an instruction whose syntax is incorrect. Usually the computer will respond to such an instruction by displaying the message: "Syntax Error" or a similar message.

```
WHAT'S WRONG?
?SYNTAX ERROR
READY
>█
```

system commands (SIS•tum kuh•MANDS) *n.* Instructions that govern operations performed by a computer's operating system, as distinct from an application program. For example, communicating with a disk drive, logging in, or listing the source code of a program would all be done using system commands.

Examples of system commands in ATARI BASIC are:

BYE	**DOS**	**NEW**
CLOAD	**ENTER**	**RUN**
CONT	**LIST**	**SAVE**
CSAVE	**LOAD**	

systems analysis (SIS•tums uh•NAL•i•sis) *n.* Studying a system being designed or one that already is working to discover the best way of using it. For example, if you had a large computer and wanted it to do a certain job for you, a systems analyst would plan the best way of making the computer do that job. This would include an outline of the programs needed to do the job and a plan of peripheral devices required.

table (TAY•bl) *n.* A collection of data organized so that any single datum within it is easy to find. Often, tables are arranged in rows and columns, so that each datum is located at the intersection of a row and a column. Thus, any datum may be identified by a row number and a column number.

talking computer (TAWK•ing kum•PYOO•tur) *n.* A computer connected to a speech synthesizer. Such a computer can send text to the speech synthesizer which converts the text to speech which you can hear.

tape (TAYP) *n.* A recording medium in the form of a long, thin strip that can be wound on a reel. Originally, the only kind of tape used by computers on which to record data was paper tape in which punched holes represented data. Now magnetic tape is used much more commonly.

tape cassette (TAYP kuh•SET) *n.* Same as cassette.

tape drive (TAYP DRIVE) *n.* A device which moves tape under control of a computer. As the tape moves, the part to be read is brought into contact with the device that reads it.

tape reader (TAYP REE•dur) *n.* A device that converts holes punched in paper tape, or magnetic fields of magnetic tape, into electrical pulses that carry data to a computer.

tape unit (TAYP YOO•nit) *n.* A device that includes a tape drive, a tape reader, and other mechanical and electronic components necessary to send data to and from tape and a computer.

task (TASK) *n.* A job to be run on a computer is said to consist of tasks. Sometimes a job is divided into tasks which are run separately, because under certain circumstances that uses less computer time.

telecommunications (TEL•uh•kuh•myoo•ni•KAY•shuns) *n.* Transmission of data over distances by electronic means. Computer data can be sent and received using any method of telecommunications: phone lines, telegraph lines or satellite relay.

teletypewriter (tel•uh•TIPE•rye•tur) *n*. An electronic device that looks like an electric typewriter. Teletypewriters are used to convert telegraph signals into written messages.

terminal (TUR•mi•nul) *n*. Technically, any device through which data is input to and/or output from a computer system. Loosely, the term usually is used to mean a combination keyboard and CRT that is used to communicate with a large computer system.

terminal symbol (TUR•mi•nul SIM•bul) *n*. When data is recorded on magnetic tape, some special character is recorded at the end of each block of data, so that the computer can keep track of where it is on the tape. These characters are called terminal symbols or terminating symbols.

terminating symbol (TUR•mi•nayt•ing SIM•bul) *n*. Same as terminal symbol.

test data (TEST DAY•tuh) *n*. Programs process data. To test whether a program runs correctly or not, test data is given to the program. The testers know what results should be produced for that data, so they can judge the program by whether or not it produces the same results.

137

testing (TEST•ing) *n.* The process of running a program under all possible conditions, with the widest possible range of input, to see whether or not it produces the results it should.

text (TEKST) *n.* Information displayed in the form of characters. Computers can display either text or graphics, using different parts of their electronics. The graphics part can display pictures of text characters, however, which are considered graphics.

text editor (TEKST ED•i•tur) *n.* A program that lets you enter text into the computer's memory and change text that is already there. Some things you can do with a text editor are delete words (or letters), insert words (or letters) and move blocks of text (one or more letters) from one place to another.

text file (TEKST FILE) *n.* Different kinds of data are processed by a computer in different ways. Therefore, the computer has to be able to tell whether a file contains text, or graphics, or a program or some other kind of data. When a file is created it is automatically labelled according to what kind of data it contains. A text file is a file that has been labelled as containing text.

thermal printer (THUR•mul PRIN•tur) *n.* A printer which uses special, heat-sensitive paper. The printer forms characters with a grid of dots, like a dot-matrix printer, but each dot is an element that may be heated. A dot is made on the paper next to each element that is hot. The virtue of thermal printers is that they make no noise.

three-dimensional (THREE–di•MEN•shun•ul) *adj.* Having width, height and depth, like a solid object. Computer displays are two-dimensional, but they can appear to be three-dimensional in the same way that the objects in a photograph or painting appear to be three-dimensional.

timesharing (TYME SHAIR•ing) *n.* The use of a computer by many different people. Usually the users are located in many places, some quite far from the computer, and communicate with it over phone lines. They are charged according to how much computer time they use. Timesharing is a way to make very large computers available to users who otherwise could not afford them.

track ball (TRAK BAWL) *n*. A device used to move the cursor around on a computer display. It consists of a mounting, usually a box, in which is set a ball. As you spin the ball, the cursor moves at the speed and in the direction of the ball's motion. Trackballs for microcomputers are used mostly with games, for example, to move a spaceship.

transaction (tran•ZAK•shun) *n*. An event that results in the creation or revision of a record in a file. For example, a program that did a company's bookkeeping might have a file for each customer, and within that file a record for each sale or purchase. Each time the company made a sale or purchase, that would be a transaction, and the program would enter a number in the appropriate record.

transistor (tran•ZIS•tur) *n*. A small electrical device that contains a semiconductor and can be used to switch an electrical circuit on and off or to amplify an electrical signal. Many computer memories are made of transistors. Transistors replaced vacuum tubes in the late nineteen fifties, allowing computers to be much smaller than they had been. Now hundreds of transistors fit in an integrated circuit.

140

transmit (tranz•MIT) *v.* To send data from one place to another.

tri-state (TRY•stayt) *adj.* An electronic component with three kinds of output. In addition to the usual outputs of high voltage and low voltage, corresponding to a binary one or zero, such devices have a third state called high-impedance, which is the same as no output at all.

turnaround time (TURN•uh•rownd TYME) *n.* The most common meaning of this term is the time it takes for a computer to do a job; that is, time between input data being given to the system, and processed data being returned.

turnkey (TURN•key) *n.* A computer system that is purchased as a unit, including software and all devices necessary to perform a job or range of jobs. The entire turnkey system is purchased from one source and is ready to operate as soon as it is installed.

turtle graphics (TUR•tl GRAF•iks) *n.* The LOGO programming language can be used to program little figures known as turtles to move about a computer display, drawing geometric shapes as they go. Toys, the size of small dogs and fitted with special pens, are also made to be programmed in LOGO and move on wheels, drawing shapes on paper spread on the floor. Both kinds of turtle graphics are used to teach geometry and computer graphics to children.

Here is an Apple screen showing a simple sequence of turtle commands:

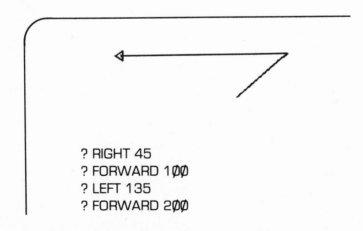

```
? RIGHT 45
? FORWARD 100
? LEFT 135
? FORWARD 200
```

two-dimensional (TOO-di•MEN•shun•ul) *adj.* Having width and height, but no depth. For example, a CRT display is two-dimensional. Computer graphics are two-dimensional, although they can appear to be three-dimensional, like a solid object.

typewriter (TIPE•rye•tur) *n.* A mechanical device used to print characters on paper with ink. Some electrical typewriters can be connected to a computer and used as printers.

unconditional branch (un•kun•DISH•uh•nul BRANCH) *n.* A program may have several parts, each of which makes the computer perform a different set of operations. When control of the computer is passed from one part of a program to another part, that is called a branch. When, at a certain point in the program a branch always occurs it is called an unconditional branch. This is the opposite of a conditional branch.

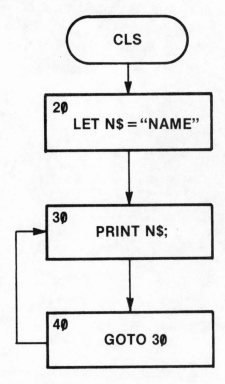

unconditional transfer (un•kun•DISH•uh•nul TRANS•fur) *n.* The same as an unconditional branch.

UNIVAC (YOO•ni•vak) *n.* Acronym for UNIVersal Automatic Computer. The first computer that was made for sale. The first one was completed in 1951 and sold to the United States Bureau of the Census. The Univac was built by the Eckert-Mauchly Computer Corporation, founded by Presper Eckert and John Mauchly, who helped build ENIAC.

universal product code (yoo•ni•VUR•sul PROD•ukt KOHD) *n.* An 11-digit computer readable code which is used in labeling retail products. The universal product code is the most widely used in the United States. The code consists of a number system character, a 5-digit manufacturer identification number and a 5-digit item code number.

upload (UP•lode) *v.* To transfer a file or block of data from a small computer to a larger one.

user (YOOZ•ur) *n.* Someone who uses a computer to perform a job. The user may not be the operator. For example, in a large system, the user may submit his program to an operator who will actually cause the computer to run the program.

user friendly (YOOZ•ur FREND•lee) *adj.* Software or hardware that is easy to use is said to be user friendly. Such software usually has menus, displays instructions for its own use, uses commands that are easy to remember, pictures instead of descriptions, etc. User friendly hardware uses devices like mice or light pens instead of the keyboard for input and is designed for physical comfort.

utility program (yoo•TIL•i•tee PROH•gram) *n.* A program that is useful in operating the computer rather than in performing a specific job. For example, a utility program might make copies of disks. The opposite of an application program.

Executing CMD "D" causes the TRSDOS (TRS-80) debugging program to load and execute.

```
100 '                    PROGRAM: DEBUG
110 ' EXAMPLE OF EXECUTION WITH DEBUG WITHIN A
      PROGRAM
120 '
130 CLS: PRINT TAB(15); "DEBUG EXAMPLE": PRINT
140 PRINT"ENTERING DEBUG"
150 FOR I = 1 TO 500: NEXT I     'DELAY A WHILE
160 '
170 ' *** ENTER DEBUGGING PACKAGE ***
180 '
190 CMD"D"
200 '
210 ' *** RETURN HERE WHEN "G" ENTER TYPED IN DEBUG ***
220 '
230 CLS: PRINT: PRINT "YOU HAVE RETURNED FROM DEBUG"
240 END
```

vacuum tube (VAK•yoom TOOB) *n.* An electric component used to switch a circuit on and off or to amplify a signal. In its simplest form, a vacuum tube has two input signals and an output signal. As one input travels through the tube and becomes the output, it can be changed by changing the voltage of the other input, which is a control input. The first computers were made out of thousands of vacuum tubes, but vacuum tubes have been replaced by transistors.

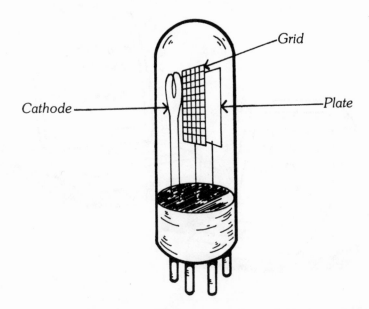

valid (VAL•id) *adj.* Acceptable to the computer. For example, each programming language has a vocabulary of commands. If the computer is running under one language, and you give it a command that is not part of that language's vocabulary, the command is not valid.

value (VAL•yoo) *n.* A word that has many specialized meanings. Generally, it means the number that something represents at the moment. For example, in logical operations, the value of a true statement is always one and the value of a false statement is always zero. The value of a variable may change. The value of a constant is always the same.

variable (VAIR•ee•uh•bul) *n.* A character or other symbol that stands for a number which may change in the course of a program. For example, the BASIC statement LET A = 5 means that whenever the computer encounters the letter A (as long as it is not in quotation marks), the computer should act as if it were the number 5. But somewhere else in the program other LET statements may change the value of A to any other number.

Everything to the left of the equal (=) sign is a variable.

VDT (VEE DEE TEE) *n.* Abbreviation for Visual Display Terminal.

video (VID•ee•oh) *n.* Loosely, another word for television, the use of electronics to send and record pictures. Video includes not only broadcast television, but also television used for industrial, educational, artistic and other purposes.

videodisk (VID•ee•oh•disk) *n.* A thin, flat, rigid disk about the size of a 33⅓ rpm phonograph record. Digital data is stored on a video disk in the form of tiny pits. A pit stands for a one, a space with no pit stands for a zero. Television pictures may be recorded digitally, as millions of ones and zeros on the disk. Most video disks are "read" by beams of laser light, and therefore never wear out.

video display (VID•ee•oh di•SPLAY) *n.* Data that appears on the screen of a video monitor, that is, a CRT.

video monitor (VID•ee•oh MON•i•tur) *n.* A CRT. When it is called a video monitor, that usually means that a video picture is being displayed on it, but a video monitor and a CRT are essentially the same thing. A television is a CRT combined with a tuner for selecting channels.

video tape (VID•ee•oh TAYP) *n.* Magnetic tape on which video pictures can be recorded. Broadcast and professional tape is usually two inches (5.08 cm), one inch (2.54 cm) or three quarters of an inch (1.91 cm) wide, although half inch (1.27 cm) tape is being used more. Video tape for home use is mostly half inch (1.27 cm), but some machines even use quarter inch (0.64 cm) tape.

video terminal (VID•ee•oh TUR•mi•nul) *n.* A terminal that includes a CRT.

visual display terminal (VIZH•oo•ul di•SPLAY TUR•mi•nul) *n.* A terminal that includes a CRT, an LCD screen or some other way of viewing data from a computer.

VLSI (VEE•EL•ES•EYE) *n.* Abbreviation for Very Large Scale Integration, the largest integrated circuits presently possible, each containing thousands of electronic components.

voice recognition unit (VOIS rek•ug•NISH•un YOO•nit) *n.* A device which converts human speech into data which the computer can use. For example, a voice recognition unit connected to a computer lets you give the computer an instruction simply by speaking it.

volatile memory (VOL•uh•til MEM•uh•ree) *n.* A kind of computer memory which keeps the data stored in it only as long as power to the computer is on. Such a memory, upon its computer being turned on, is always blank.

wafer (WAY•fur) *n*. A thin, flat piece of substance, usually silicon, on which integrated circuits can be made.

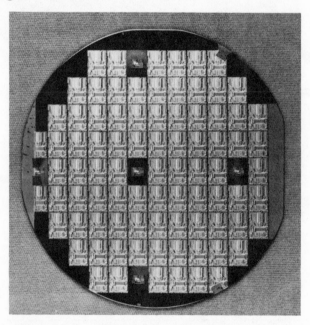

word (WURD) *n*. The smallest amount of data that a computer usually treats as a single unit. Addresses in a computer's memory are one word apart. In most microcomputers words are one or two bytes long.

word processing (WURD PROS•es•ing) *n*. Using a computer to write and alter documents and other writing. Word processing provides capabilities in addition to those available with text editing, such as margin justification, automatic page numbering, automatic headings, etc.

write (RITE) *v.* When a device sends data to another device, we say that it is writing to that device. For example, a computer writes data to a disk.

write protected (RITE proh•TEK•tud) *n.* A medium to which it is impossible to send data. For example, most disks have a small slot cut out of one side of their cover. If that disk is covered with opaque tape, the disk drive cannot send magnetic signals to that disk and therefore cannot change the data on it. Likewise, a file on a disk may include data that tells the computer not to write to it.

HANDBOOK

CONTENTS

COMPUTER HARDWARE

How A Computer Works

A computer is not a single machine, but a number of machines connected to each other. When a computer does a job, each of the machines does a part of the job. Because computers are not one thing, but many things working together, we often call them computer systems.

A computer system consists of a CPU connected to a number of peripheral devices. What those peripherals are may differ from system to system. A microcomputer system used to keep track of the family budget may consist of a central processor, memory, a keyboard, a disk drive and a monitor. (If these terms are not familiar to you, don't worry; we are just getting started, and you will understand them all before we are through. Or, if you wish, you may consult the dictionary section of this book where they are defined.)

A large, main frame computer used to design aircraft might include a central processor and memory which in both cases would be much larger than the microcomputer's. In addition, it might contain keyboards, card readers, terminals, data links, printers, plotters, disk drives, tape drives and perhaps other devices as well.

The central processor, or central processing unit, or CPU is the part that controls everything a computer does. (It goes by more than one name. That is true of many things in the world of computers. Sometimes all the names become confusing, but don't let that bother you. After awhile you will learn what they all are, and everything will seem much simpler than at first.)

The CPU, as we will call it, is itself composed of several parts, as we will see later. Right now, just remember that this is typical of computers: a system is composed of parts, these parts are composed of parts, and those parts are in turn composed of even smaller parts, and so on. This pyramid of parts is called a hierarchy. Now the smallest parts in a hierarchy - the parts at the lowest level - can be very simple and easy to understand; yet the entire system - the highest level of hierarchy - may be large and complicated. Therefore, we will start with the smallest parts and work our way upwards.

Data

The CPU does only two things: it transfers numbers from one place to the other, and it adds, subtracts, multiplies and divides them. (See, pretty simple!) Yet the CPU is the "brain" of the entire computer system. How can a computer system be used to design a jumbo jet when all it can do is move numbers around? To answer that question we must understand what data is. (It is common in the computer world to use the word 'data' to mean many data or one datum, but we will stick to the proper English usage.)

The most common kind of communication among people is speech. When people speak to each other they pass information in the form of words. Words are strung together in sentences, and each sentence carries one or more ideas. Words are made up of sounds. A word like 'elementary' has many sounds in it. A word like 'a' has only one sound. Sounds are a kind of data. We could make a lot of sounds that are not words, as babies do before they learn to speak. We cannot understand what a baby is trying to tell us because a baby cannot put data together so that they carry information.

Computers generally do not use spoken words as data. Instead, computers use numbers. Computers use numbers to stand for all kinds of information. This is called encoding.

Computers code information into numbers. This is quite simple. We use codes all the time. For example, when we select channel seven on the television set we are actually telling the television to show us the program being broadcast on a certain signal with a different frequency than any of the other signals in the air. Seven is just a code for that frequency.

It is much easier to remember the number seven than to remember, say, 80.2 kilohertz. It also takes less space on the dial. In the television set, 80.2 kilohertz is encoded as the number seven. Similarly, all information inside the computer is represented by numbers, but not numbers we are used to. Computers use a special kind of number called binary.

Binary Arithmetic

A computer is made out of thousands or millions of electronic circuits. An electronic circuit is a path in which electrons flow. If the path is interrupted, electrons cannot flow along it. An interrupted path is called an open circuit. A flashlight is a simple electronic circuit. When the switch is off, the circuit is open; no electrons flow and the bulb gives no light.

Generally speaking, a circuit can be in one of two states: open or closed, on or off. Therefore, the best number system for use in the computer is one that has only two digits, instead of the ten we are used to. Such a system is called the binary, or base two, system. It has only two digits: one and zero. (On and off, closed and open.) But how can ones and zeros by themselves serve as a number system?

Let's take the number 250. This is a decimal number, the kind we are used to, which uses the digits zero through nine. As we all know, the zero means no ones, the five means five tens or fifty and the two means two hundreds. The rightmost column represents ones, the next column tens, the next hundreds and so on. Each column has a value ten times that of the one before it.

In binary numbers, each column has a value two times that of the one before it. The rightmost column stands for ones, the next for twos, the next for fours and so on. Therefore, the binary number 1 is the same as decimal 1. But the binary number 10 (pronounced one-zero) is decimal two, and binary 11 is decimal three.

Let's take the binary number 11111010. We have one 128, one 64, one 32, one 16, one 8, no 4's, one 2 and no 1's. That adds up to the decimal number 250. Binary 11111010 is the same number as decimal 250. 11111010 is a code for 250!

The rules for adding binary numbers are actually quite simple. Two zeros add up to zero, and one plus zero equals one, just as in decimal numbers. One plus one is zero with a one to carry. To understand this, remember that in binary, 2 is written 10. Three binary ones add up to one with a 1 to carry: decimal three is binary 11.

Boolean Algebra

One of the important things you can do with binary numbers is called Boolean algebra. Boolean algebra is a way of expressing logic with numbers. By logic we mean truth and falsehood. It may sound complex, but the idea is simple: if something is true it is represented by a one, and if it is not true it is represented by a zero.

The statement "one plus one is two" is a true statement, so it would be represented by a one. The statement "two plus two is five" would be represented by a zero. We can do some clever tricks with this simple idea. Take the two statements together: "one plus one is two and two plus two is five". In Boolean terms, this would be called an AND statement. It would be written in Boolean algebra as 1 (the true statement) × 0 (the false statement) = 0.

How do we know the answer is zero? Because Boolean algebra is a set of rules that tell us what the answers to such problems are. Boolean algebra's elementary functions, in addition to the AND function, are the OR, NAND and NOR functions. In each case, Boolean rules tell us what we get when we have different combinations of truth and falsehood.

Boolean algebra is actually a large, complex system within mathematics, but it is all built on the simple idea we have just seen. (Does a complicated system built out of simple parts sound familiar?) One of the most useful things that a computer does is called conditional branching, and it is possible because of Boolean algebra. We will say more about that later.

Electronic Data

Now that we understand data, binary arithmetic and encoding, let's put them all together. How does a computer encode data as binary numbers?

We will look at one kind of information: text. Text is writing, and includes words, numbers and other symbols. We call these characters. "q" is a character. "Q" is another character. All of the following symbols are characters: 1 " j @ < ?   H o 0 .. Numbers and letters are called alphanumeric characters. Each character can be represented by a code.

The most common computer code for characters is called the ASCII code, usually referred to simply as ASCII (AS•kee). In ASCII, the numbers 0 through 9 are encoded as binary 110000 through binary 111001. The upper case letters A through Z are 1000001 through 1011010. The question mark is 111111; the plus sign is 101011; and so forth.

What this means is that whenever you hit a key on a computer keyboard, the corresponding binary number is sent to the computer's CPU. As long as that character is inside the computer, it is in the form of a binary code. ASCII codes stand not only for characters, but for certain functions as well.

For example, if you hold down the control key and then press G on many microcomputers, the ASCII code 111 will be sent to the CPU, which will beep the computer's little loudspeaker very briefly. If you press the RETURN key, the ASCII code 1101 will cause a carriage return.

Input/Output/Processing

We said earlier that the only things a CPU does is move numbers from place to place and change them arithmetically. A computer system does only three things: it inputs data, processes data and outputs data.

An ASCII code sent from the keyboard to the CPU is one example of computer input. Input simply means data going into a device, whether the device is a computer's CPU, a CRT, a disk drive or anything else.

What goes in may also come out, and data coming out of a device is called output. Data going from the keyboard to the CPU is output from the keyboard, but the same data is input to the CPU. When discussing input and output you have to be careful to keep track of which is which.

Processing is what the CPU does. Processing data simply means changing it or transferring it from one place to another.

Let's say you are playing a game on a computer. The game involves moving a starship around on the screen of a CRT. Let's say that you move the starship up by pressing the I key, down by pressing the M key, left with the J key and right with the K key.

When you press one of those keys, you are sending input to the CPU. The CPU receives the code for either I,J,K or M. In response, it sends out other signals to the CRT. We say that it has processed the data from the keyboard into different data. That new data becomes output. When the new output reaches the monitor, it causes the starship to move.

So all input, processing and output involves sending data from one place to another, but how is that done?

Electronic Signals

We have already seen that keyboard strokes are converted into ASCII code. A keyboard consists of more than just the keys which you see. Below those keys are special electronics, on a printed circuit board. These electronics convert each keystroke into an electronic signal.

An electronic signal is a flow of electrons in a special pattern. Think of a crowded freeway, full of cars. If the freeway were a big circle, it would be like an electronic circuit, and the cars would be like electrons; they would keep going around the circuit. (We are using imaginary cars that never run out of gas.)

Now if a stop light were placed at some point in the circuit, we could control the cars. If we made the light go red, the cars approaching it would stop, and all the cars behind them would have to stop, and pretty soon, no cars would be moving. The circuit would be open; no electrons would be flowing.

Now let's say that we give the cars a green light for one second and then a red light for one second and then a green light again, and so on. Pretty soon we would have cars leaving the light in little groups, with spaces in between them. By changing the timing of the light, we could change the spaces between groups of cars.

Let's say we decided that each group of cars would always have a small gap behind it, say fifteen feet. And let's say we decide that after that fifteen foot gap we may have either another group of cars or a gap of a hundred feet. By turning the light on and off, we could chop the flow of cars into alternating units of cars and large gaps. Or we could have two groups of cars followed by a gap. Or three gaps, followed by a group of cars, then another gap, then two groups of cars. In fact, we could create any pattern of cars and gaps that we wanted to create.

Suppose that a group of cars stands for a one, and a large gap stands for a zero. Do you see that we could use the light to create a binary code? That is exactly what is done by the keyboard electronics. Each time a keystroke is pressed, the traffic light is turned on and off a certain number of times, and as a result, a flow of electrons is sent out that has a certain pattern to it. That is called an electronic signal, and it can carry a binary code, including ASCII.

Whenever data is transferred from one place to another, within a computer system, it is transferred in the form of electronic signals. Technically, the signals consist of patterns of electrons, but it is much easier to think of data transfer as lots of little ones and zeros zipping through wires between one part of the computer system and another.

Timing

The ones and zeros travelling around inside computer systems travel at the speed of light, and millions of them are on the move at a time. How does the computer keep track of all these signals? The answer is, with a clock!

Think of our example of the freeway full of cars. If the cars are going by in a pattern that carries a code, we must have some way of reading the code. Let's imagine that we put a person next to the freeway with a pad and pencil. As traffic goes by he writes down a one for every group of cars and a zero for every gap. It takes him a certain amount of time to write numbers down, and we do not want him to miss any.

So let's say that we want him to look up at the beginning of every group of cars or gap. We may do this by attaching a clock to a buzzer and to the traffic light. Once a minute, the clock will allow the light to change and will ring the buzzer. The light may change once a minute, or it may stay the same, but it may only change at the same time as the buzzer rings. The man may only look up when the buzzer rings.

As a result, the man will look up often enough so that he will be able to count every group of cars, or gap between groups, that goes by. We call this synchronization. The man and the cars and the light are all synchronized by the clock.

Computers work in a similar way. Every CPU contains an electrical component called an oscillator. An oscillator puts out regular electronic pulses, just like our traffic clock, but much faster. Instead of once a minute, computer clocks (oscillators) send out millions of pulses a second! Everything that happens inside a computer is synchronized by the clock. As you can see, computers can handle a very huge number of electronic signals in a very brief time.

How Data Is Processed

Before we can understand how the CPU actually processes data, we should know something about how the insides of a computer are arranged and how the different parts work.

Three kinds of computers exist: main frames, minis and micros. Main frames are the largest, fastest and most powerful; they have the largest memories, the most rapid clocks and can do many jobs at the same time. A typical main frame computer system would fill a large truck.

Minis are the middle-sized computers. They are a little slower, a little smaller and a little less powerful than main frames. An average mini would fill a van.

Micros are the smallest computers. Most microcomputer systems would fit in the trunk of a small car. However, changes in technology are blurring the differences among computers. Almost no difference exists between the largest minis and the smallest main frames, and between the largest micros and the smallest minis.

The simplest kind of computer is the micro. A microcomputer system such as you would use as a home computer might consist of a CPU, memory and keyboard in one unit, a CRT, a disk drive, a small printer and a pair of game paddles. We will use this typical home computer as an example.

Inside our home computer is a large printed circuit board. Soldered to it are a few dozen sockets into which chips may be plugged. It also holds many small components: resistors, capacitors and others, and several long slots, into which interface boards may be plugged. Somewhere it contains small jacks for the CRT cable and for a cassette tape player/recorder. It is called the motherboard.

The motherboard contains the CPU, the internal memory, input/output ports and busses which connect all of these parts. Let's look at each of these.

The Memory

Every computer must have a place to store data. Some of this data is used frequently, for example, programs that are "built in" to a computer and which control its most fundamental operations. (We will say more about this in the section on instruction sets.) This memory is called ROM, and the data it stores is there permanently.

Most of a computer's memory, however, is used to store data temporarily. This kind of memory is called RAM. The part of a computer's memory made up of RAM is called main memory, internal memory or temporary storage. (Disks, tape and other media for keeping data for a long time are called mass storage or auxiliary storage.)

A computer's memory is composed of thousands of cells. In our home computer, each cell is a special kind of electronic component. This component is called a flip-flop. The CPU can put either a one or a zero into a flip-flop and it will stay there, going around and around in the flip-flop until the CPU changes it. In larger computers, memory cells may be made out of something other than flip-flops, for instance magnetic cores.

A single one or zero is called a bit, which is an acronym for BInary digiT. Each flip-flop can hold one bit of information. Our typical home computer moves data in groups of eight bits at a time. Eight bits are called a byte. A byte is enough bits to hold any ASCII code, so we often say that a byte is the same as a character, though that is not technically true.

(Four bits are called a nybble, but we do not have to worry about that.) The memory in our typical home computer can hold 65,536 bytes of data. We call this 64K of memory. The K stands for kilo, which means one thousand.

Of course 65,536 is more than 64,000. Computer memory is built in chunks, usually chunks of 4096 bytes. The smallest memory a home computer might have is 4096 bytes, or 4K. The next largest memory would usually be 16K (16389). No computer would have a memory of, say, 5,000 or 4,000. So it does not cause confusion to call 65,536 64K.

RAM and ROM

As we saw above, computer memory is divided into two kinds, RAM and ROM. These terms refer to what the memory does, not what it is made of. The data in RAM memory can be changed at any time, but the data in ROM memory is put in once, normally before the computer is assembled, and it is not changed after that.

ROM, by the way, stands for Read Only Memory, since the computer can read data out of the ROM, but cannot write new data into it. RAM stands for Random Access Memory, which means that data in any part of the RAM can be read as quickly as that in any other part.

Addressing

That brings us to the question, how *does* the computer find data in memory?

Let's use our 64K memory home computer as an example. Each of these 65,536 bytes is actually a cluster of eight flip-flops. Each cluster is called a memory location, and each one is given a number, from 0 to 65,535. (In the computer world, numbering almost always starts at 0 instead of one.) The number of a memory location is called its address. The computer is built so that the CPU can send a byte of data to any memory address or fetch a byte of data from any memory address.

In other words, a computer's main memory is like thousands of little boxes, each containing a byte of data. Each box has a number, and the CPU can transfer a byte to or from any box, according to its number.

This memory is organized into regions. In our home computer it might be divided up into a dozen or more regions, each one set aside for a different kind of data. For example, addresses 0 to 255 might be one region, addresses 256 to 511 the next, addresses 1024 to 4095 the next, and so on, until the whole 64K was divided into regions.

A list of which addresses are located in which regions is called a memory map. The memory could be pictured as a large box, marked off into smaller boxes to represent each region. (And each region would contain the even smaller boxes to represent single memory locations.) Such a picture would be a diagram of the memory map. Most computer manuals include some form of memory map to show where in the memory different kinds of data are put.

So what kind of data does the computer keep in these regions, anyway? The answer is, two kinds: program data and storage data.

Program Data

A program is a series of instructions which tell the computer to do things. We will say more about programs in section three of this handbook. For now, you just need to know that the instructions which make up a program are entered into the computer in the form of data.

Each instruction consists of one or more bytes of data. A program is stored in memory. Our home computer sets aside two large regions on its memory map for programs.

Remember that a computer cannot do anything by itself. It can only work in response to instructions. That goes even for things it does all the time. For example, a CPU can only transfer data from one place to another under the direction (we say control) of a program. The things that a computer must do to be able to work are controlled by a group of programs called its operating system. In our home computer, most of the operating system is kept in ROM.

One part, which controls the transfer of data to and from disks, is called the Disk Operating System, or DOS. DOS is kept on a disk and loaded into main memory each time the computer is turned on. It is put in one of the two regions in the memory map that are reserved for programs.

The other program region is for programs loaded in by the user. These programs may direct the computer to do any number of things, from word processing to game playing to writing new programs. Normally, you do not need to know where things are put in memory, so you do not need to pay attention to the memory map. But if you are writing your own program, you need to know where the computer will put it in memory.

The memory map is only a guide, and under certain circumstances the computer uses the same region for more than one kind of data. Therefore, unless you make sure to avoid it, the computer might put your program in memory, and then put some other data in the same place, erasing part of your program. Once that happens your program will not work. When this happens, we say that the program has been "clobbered".

Storage Data

Any data in memory that is not part of a program instruction, is called storage data. This includes many different kinds of data. The two main kinds of data which we may want to store in our home computer are strings and variables.

A string is a group of characters always treated as a single unit. For example, the word 'computer' is a string consisting of eight characters. The expression '1234' is a string of four characters. Now, the string '1234' is not the same as the number 1234, as far as the computer is concerned. Remember that a string must always be treated as a whole. To be able to do anything worthwhile with a number, such as add, subtract, multiply or divide it, you must be able to break it into parts and change the parts around. That is why a computer cannot calculate with a number that is expressed as a string. When you are using a computer, you must tell it whether a group of numerical characters is a string or a number.

A variable is one kind of number in a computer's memory. Actually, a variable is a special memory address which you have reserved and given a label. Let's say you give address 13123 the label 'Mice' as part of a program which counts mice going through a maze. The number of mice that have gone through will be kept at that memory address (and the following addresses as the number grows.) Each time a mouse goes through, the number will change. That is, the number kept at the location 'Mice' will vary. This number is called a variable.

Central Processing Unit (CPU)

Besides the memory, the other major part of the motherboard is the Central Processing Unit, or CPU. The CPU is the "brains" of the computer. Some people refer to the entire motherboard as the CPU, but when we say CPU we mean the processing circuitry by itself, apart from internal memory or power supply. In our home computer, the entire CPU is in a single integrated circuit, called a microprocessor. In larger computers, the CPU may consist of more than one microprocessor, or even of one or more printed circuit boards.

The CPU controls everything that a computer system does. Yet, as we saw earlier, the CPU does only two things: it moves numbers from one place to another and it performs arithmetic operations on those numbers. (By arithmetic operations we mean addition, subtraction, multiplication and division.)

The numbers it moves are binary numbers; that is, groups of ones and zeros. Later on, in the section on instruction sets, we will see how the CPU can repeat the only two things it does in different combinations to perform complicated tasks. Right now we will see how the CPU in our home computer is constructed.

The way that the parts of a computer are put together is often called its architecture. That goes for the CPU as well. CPU architecture consists of various parts put together in a certain way. In our home computer these parts are the clock, tiny memory cells called registers, an Arithmetic-Logic Unit (ALU) where the arithmetic operations take place, an instruction-decoder, and timer. We have already seen how the clock works. It consists of an oscillator and some related circuitry which make regular timing pulses available to the computer system. Everything that happens in the computer happens in step with the clock.

Registers

The registers are usually labeled with letters: for example the A register, the B and C registers, the PC register. Some of these labels stand for functions - PC stands for Program Counter - and some do not. Registers are used to store small amounts of data, usually for brief amounts of time. In our home computer, each register can hold one byte of data, that is, eight bits, any of which may be either a one or a zero. This data comes from memory.

When the CPU moves a binary number from one place to another, it must pass through the CPU itself. That is one thing that the registers do: hold numbers that are just passing through. Registers also hold numbers while they are being added, subtracted, multiplied or divided. For example, one register is called the accumulator (also called the A register). When the ALU performs an arithmetic operation, it stores the result in the accumulator.

The PC register is used to keep track of where the computer is in a program. The number in the PC register is the address in memory of the program instruction currently being executed. The PC counter is automatically changed after each instruction to the address of the next instruction.

Then the CPU knows where to look for the next instruction. This may seem a roundabout way of doing things, and in a way it is. Computers work this way for a good reason which we do not have space to explain. Just remember that the CPU cannot use any number that is not held somewhere in the CPU itself - in one of the registers.

The Arithmetic Logic Unit (ALU)

The ALU also contains registers, but fewer registers than the rest of the CPU does. When the ALU is going to perform an arithmetic operation on two numbers, it puts each of them in one of its registers. It can also store the result of an arithmetic operation in one of its own registers, or it can send it to the accumulator.

How does the ALU perform arithmetic operations? Let's say it wants to add two numbers: 11010110 and 01001110. Remember the rules of binary addition . . .

$$11010110$$
$$\underline{01001110}$$
$$100100100$$

You may wonder, if a register only holds eight bits, how can it hold the result of this addition?

The answer is, it can't. So the ALU uses another register to remember whether the result has an extra one as its most significant digit (the one furthest to your left). This other register is called a status register. It may have eight bits, or it may have fewer than that. In either case, only one of those bits needs to be set to remember whether or not the result of an arithmetic operation is too big to fit in the accumulator. That bit has its own name. It is called the Carry bit, since it is set to a one whenever the result of an arithmetic operation carries over into an extra digit.

The ALU performs all arithmetic operations, and it can also perform what are called logic operations. A logic operation simply applies the rules of Boolean algebra to given statements. For instance, a program may wish to turn on a heater if the temperature is too low. A thermostat would be attached to the computer, and it would periodically send a number to the CPU, a zero if the room were warm enough, a one if it were too cold.

Each time this happened, the program would then tell the CPU to send a signal to turn on the heater if the number it just received were a one. The ALU would decide if the number were a one or not. It would do this by subtracting it from a one. If the answer were zero, it would know it had a one. If the answer were one, it would know it had received a zero from the thermostat. In this way, the ALU can receive inputs of ones and zeros, and provide outputs corresponding to actions the computer is supposed to take.

Instruction Decoder

Of course, to know what actions it is supposed to take, the computer must be able to read a program. To do this the CPU depends on an Instruction Decoder.

The Instruction Decoder is the traffic operations center of the CPU, and therefore, of the whole computer system. We have seen that both data and program instructions are constantly being sent to the CPU. The Instruction Decoder decides whether incoming signals represent the next program instruction or whether they represent data.

If a signal is data, the Instruction Decoder sends it to the register or other location indicated by the previous program instruction. The Instruction Decoder is, in turn, regulated by the clock. It knows that program instructions will come in on certain clock beats, and that data comes in on others.

Busses and Control

We have talked a lot about data and program instructions flitting about inside the computer at amazing speeds. Now we will say a little bit about the routes taken by this dizzying exchange of signals among memory, CPU and input/output ports (of which more in a moment).

Of course, like all electronic signals, the pulses which carry ones and zeros from place to place within a computer run through metal lines, whether wires, strips of metal printed on a board, or microscopic conductors within an integrated circuit. Groups of these pathways carry certain kinds of information to every part of the computer. Some carry only signals that stand for memory addresses. Others carry only data. These are known respectively as the address bus and the data bus.

Simply put, what a bus does is make the data it carries available everywhere in the system. For example, let's say the CPU wanted to send a number to memory location 9999. It would send the number out on the data bus and the memory location out on the address bus. All memory locations would be exposed to the number, but only the location whose address was on the address line would let the number in.

Input/Output

Input/Output, or I/O, refers to data sent or received by the CPU, to or from any device other than internal memory, including the keyboard, the CRT, mass storage, etc.

Ports

Data is sent to and from peripheral devices, including mass storage, through ports. Physically, a port may be any of several kinds of connections: a slot for an interface card, a plug for a CRT cable, a socket for pins connected to a ribbon cable, etc. All ports are the same, however, in that they can be addressed. In other words, the CPU can send data to a port in the same way that it sends data to a memory location. Each port has a number which the CPU treats as an address.

Handshaking

When the CPU sends data to a peripheral, it sends it at a certain rate of speed. Some devices, such as a printer, cannot use the data as fast as it comes in, so it must send data back to the computer every once in a while, telling it to stop sending data temporarily. This process is like two people speaking on walkie talkies such that when one is done talking he must say "over" or something like it, to let the other know that he may start talking.

With computers, this process of keeping the data flowing smoothly is called handshaking. Various standards have been worked out, so that a peripheral may talk back to a computer. These standards are referred to as communications protocols.

PERIPHERALS

So exactly what kind of devices are we talking about when we discuss I/O? We have already mentioned some. Let's learn a little more about them, and about some new ones as well.

Mass Storage

The heaviest exchange of data is with mass storage. By mass storage, we mean a way of storing data permanently, in much larger amounts than will fit in the computer's internal memory. The mass storage for our home computer is on diskettes, thin disks of plastic coated with magnetizable material. Ones and zeros can be recorded on a disk as the presence or absence of a magnetic field at a specific location. Therefore, to be useful, the disk must be divided into hundreds of thousands of these locations, each one ready to hold one bit of data. For a typical home computer, the number of bits on a disk might be a million and a quarter or more (roughly 150,000 bytes).

A brand new, blank disk, however, has no locations. It is just a uniform layer of metal oxide, waiting to be magnetized. That is why every new disk must be initialized by the computer before it can be used. In initializing a disk, the computer defines data paths on the disk called tracks. A typical home diskette might have 30 to 40 tracks, concentric rings around the center of the disk, each one closer than the last to the disk's outer edge.

Each track is, in turn, divided into sectors, and each sector can hold a certain amount of data, say 256 bytes. The computer defines tracks and sectors by recording numbers on the disk at evenly spaced intervals. In effect, these numbers are addresses on the disk. They allow the computer to record data on a disk, record that data's address on another part of the disk, called a directory, and find that data at a later date.

Disk Drive Architecture

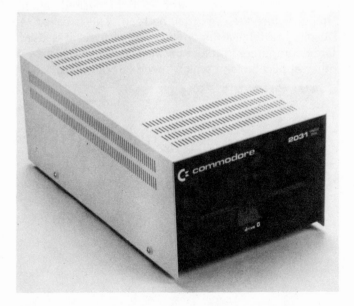

A disk drive is the device which actually writes data onto the disk and reads it off of the disk. A disk drive consists of three parts: the controller, the motor and the head.

In our home computer, the controller is a printed circuit card which fits into a slot on the motherboard. The head is a tiny electromagnet, like that on any tape recorder, placed so that it is right next to the disk. It can be moved in and out from the center of the disk. This motion, combined with the spinning of the disk, can put any point on the disk directly under the head. If the head receives an electrical pulse from the controller it becomes a magnet, and the point beneath it on the disk becomes magnetized.

The controller receives data from the CPU. It sends this data to the head, at the same time sending signals to the motor so that the correct points pass under the head at the correct time to receive data. The result is a stream of ones and zeros recorded onto the disk where the controller wants them. Reading data from a disk follows the same steps in reverse, with the head acting as a pickup.

Since almost any point on the surface of the disk may be positioned almost immediately under the head, any bit of data may be read as quickly as any other. This is called random access.

Tape

Data may also be recorded on tape, but it will not be random access. Obviously, with a tape, the entire tape up to the desired data must pass over the head, before the data may be read. This is called sequential access. Despite the relative inconvenience of tape, it is used a great deal on large computers to make backup copies of the data on disks, and for other applications in which speed is not critical.

Displays

A display is simply a device which makes data from a computer visible. Most displays make use of a cathode ray tube (CRT), but some use liquid crystal displays (LCD), like the display on a digital watch, or some other kind of visual medium.

All displays use some kind of cursor, a character such as a small rectangle or an underline, which shows a person where on the screen he is presently working. For example, if you are typing data into a computer, and the text you type is being displayed at the same time, as you type, the cursor moves across the screen. Each time you type a character it appears where the cursor used to be, and the cursor moves one space to your right.

CRTs

A CRT is a picture tube used in televisions to convert a stream of electrons into a picture. The same kind of tube is used to display pictures and text from a computer. For text, the screen of a CRT is divided into vertical columns and horizontal rows. A typical CRT for a home computer has about 25 rows and either 40 or 80 columns of text. For pictures, a typical home computer might have in the area of two hundred or more rows and three hundred or more columns.

A CRT used as a display for a microcomputer, such as our home computer, is often called a monitor. It lets you monitor data from the computer.

Video Display Terminals

A video display terminal (VDT) is a CRT display and a keyboard all in the same unit. In other words, a VDT allows a person and a computer to communicate with each other. Some VDTs are referred to as dumb, and others as smart. A smart VDT is one that can perform some processing on its own. A dumb VDT can only display data from the computer and send data to it, and has no ability to process that data.

VDTs are used with large computers. One such computer may be connected to several, or even dozens of VDTs. At each VDT a person may be performing a different task, running a different program. The CPUs of such computers are able to share their time among all the terminals.

Keyboards

The keyboard of a computer is also a peripheral device, and data travels between keyboard and CPU through an I/O port. In our home computer, the keyboard may be built into the same unit that contains the CPU and internal memory, or it may be separate, connected to the CPU by cable. The keyboard is the primary way for you to send data to the computer.

Printers

Printers receive data from a computer and write it on paper. A number of methods are used to do this.

Impact printers use a ribbon, much as a typewriter. Some mechanism strikes the ribbon to transfer a character to paper. This mechanism may be a raised version of the character set on a daisy wheel, type ball or print thimble. Or it may be an arrangement of tiny rods that print a letter made out of dots. This is called dot matrix printing.

Some impact printers can print an entire line of text at a time. These use a row of wheels. Each wheel holds all the characters of the alphabet. When all the wheels are lined up to type a line of text, the whole row of wheels is pressed against the ribbon. Line printers are faster than other kinds of impact printers, but usually type only upper case letters.

Electrostatic printers, unlike impact printers, are quiet. They print by putting electrical charges on the paper in a dot matrix. Fine particles of dried ink are then shaken onto the paper, and stick only to the charged points, thus forming letters.

Thermal printers are also silent. They print characters in the same way as early copying machines, with heated elements in the shape of a dot matrix. Thermal printers are very quiet, but require specially treated paper.

Plotters

A plotter is used to convert data from a computer into pictures and diagrams. Some dot matrix printers can do this too, but not as efficiently as a plotter that is designed to do nothing else.

All plotters use x,y coordinates, also known as Cartesian coordinates after the seventeenth century mathematician, Descartes. Cartesian coordinates are used to identify points on a flat surface. If the width of a surface, called the x-axis, is divided into points, say, 1 to 1000, and so is the height, the y-axis, then every point on the surface may be identified as the intersection of two lines, one drawn through some point on the width, and another on the height.

For instance, the point at the center of the surface would have the coordinates 500,500. (We always give the x coordinate first.) This is the same method we use to locate a town on a road map. A plotter does the same thing, but once it finds the point it makes a mark there. Since any picture can be formed by enough dark points on a light background, as are photos in your newspaper, a plotter can convert a

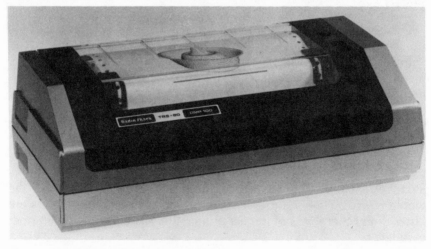

stream of x and y coordinates into a picture.

Plotters also can draw lines using x,y coordinates to locate the lines on paper.

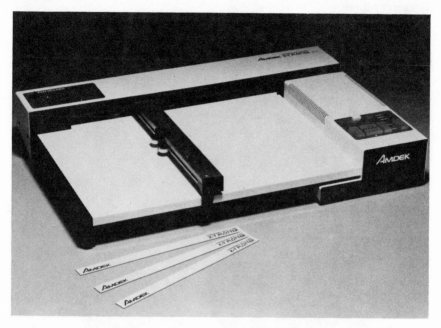

Digitizing Tablets

A digitizing tablet is the reverse of a plotter. Instead of converting Cartesian coordinates into points on a surface, it converts points on a surface into Cartesian coordinates.

A digitizing tablet, or graphics tablet as it is sometimes called, is a flat surface connected to a pointer of some kind. The pointer can be placed at any location on the tablet, and the tablet will send the Cartesian coordinates of that location to the computer. This allows you to draw by hand a picture which can be stored and processed by the computer.

Light Pens

A light pen is used in conjunction with a CRT. A light pen looks like a slightly oversized ball point pen. At its tip is a lens. The light pen is held up to the display on a CRT and "sees" what is there. It sends data describing what it sees back to the computer, and the computer can tell where on the CRT the light pen is pointing. Light pens are used to move cursors on a display and to tell the computer where to change something in the display. They can also be used to draw directly on the display, but they cannot do that as quickly or as accurately as a digitizing tablet.

Paddles

Paddles are used to move objects in a display. Paddles come in sets of two. One paddle moves things along the x-axis and the other moves things along the y-axis. Paddles are used only with home computers, mostly for playing games. Each paddle has a knob and one or more buttons. As the knob is turned, an object in the display moves. The buttons are used to do things like fire guns in combat games.

Joysticks

Essentially, a joystick is two paddles in one device. Instead of knobs, a joystick has a lever mounted on a ball joint. The lever can be moved in any direction. An object on a display will move in the same direction. Thus, with a joystick you can make an object move not only vertically and horizontally, but diagonally as well.

Like paddles, joysticks are used to play games on home computers. However, they are also used as important parts of large computer systems, in industrial design and other applications.

Track Balls

A track ball is used for purposes similar to that of a joystick. A track ball is a sphere mounted in a box, so that part of it is outside the box. Two rollers are placed perpendicularly to each other and touching the ball. Depending on which direction the ball is turned, one or both of the rollers will turn as well. Their movement is translated into motion on a display screen. A true track ball can control not only the direction of movement of a character on the screen, but its speed as well. Not all home computers can use a track ball to control speed, however.

Mice

A mouse is really a track ball upside down. Instead of turning the track ball with your hand, you run the mouse over a hard surface. Some kinds of mice require a special surface marked off in grid lines. Most mice, like other controllers, contain buttons for controlling on-off functions, like firing a phaser in a space game or selecting an item from a menu.

Voice Recognition / Synthesis Devices

Some kinds of data may be input to and output from a computer system by human voice. Voice recognition devices convert spoken instructions into electronic signals to the computer. Voice synthesis devices convert signals from a computer into synthetic speech which a human can hear and understand. Voice devices are still very limited, especially for home computers.

HISTORY OF THE COMPUTER

Humans have used devices to help them calculate since before we began to record our history. No doubt the first calculating device was our fingers. Then came simple scratches in the ground, or rows of stones to keep track of numbers being calculated. As calculations became more complicated, early mechanisms were developed.

Perhaps the oldest of these still in use is the abacus. An abacus consists of beads strung on rods or wires. Someone who is good at using one can add, subtract, multiply and divide long numbers very quickly by moving the beads to keep track of numbers at different steps during the calculation. Abacuses have been used for at least 2500 years, and are still used in many parts of the world.

For centuries, calculating devices were no more complicated than the abacus. But after the Renaissance in Europe, science, commerce and manufacturing began to advance quickly. By the seventeenth century, mathematics had become an important tool for solving the problems met in these and other activities. As mathematical problems became more complicated, especially after the discoveries of trigonometry and calculus, some scientists started thinking about how to use a machine to do calculations which took people a long time to do, and at which people made mistakes.

In the seventeenth century, two mathematicians invented the earliest of such machines. In France, Blaise Pascal built a machine which could add numbers. The machine had several wheels, with the digits 0 through 9 on them. If you turned some of the wheels to the two numbers you wished to add, other wheels would automatically be turned so as to display the result. In Germany, Gottfried Leibniz built a similar machine which could multiply as well as add, but it did not always work.

The next great inventor of calculating machines was Charles Babbage, an Englishman who worked in the first half of the nineteenth century. Babbage contributed more to the history of computers as a thinker than as an inventor, because most of the calculating machines he thought up were never built. He did, however, build one machine that worked, and he was the first person to envision the basic parts that a computer must have.

The working machine that Babbage built he called a Difference Engine. It could add bigger numbers with more accuracy than Pascal's earlier machine, but it was still crude by our standards. Babbage's thoughts about what parts a true computer must have were not at all crude. He was the first person to think of a calculating machine as having input/output, an ALU (he called it a mill), a means of transferring data within the machine (busses today, but meshed mechanical gears in his machines) and a memory (he called it a store, whence our term 'storage').

Babbage also recognized the necessity of conditional operations; that is, he saw that no important automatic calculations can be done unless the machine can choose the route a calculation will take, depending on a result part way through the calculation.

Finally, Babbage borrowed an idea from the French inventor, Joseph Jacquard. Jacquard had devised a way of punching holes in cards, and using these cards as part of a mechanism to control a loom. As different cards, with different patterns of holes passed through the mechanism, the pattern woven into the cloth changed accordingly. In effect, the loom was programmed with punched cards. Babbage was the first person to see that this method could be used to program a calculating machine.

George Boole, inventor of Boolean algebra, lived in England at the same time as Babbage. During Boole's life, Boolean algebra was never applied to mechanical calculators. Until decades later, Boolean algebra was only a branch of mathematics. Adapted to computers, Boolean algebra is used to analyze and manipulate data in a large number of ways.

Herman Hollerith was working for the United States census in 1880, and saw that a lot of time could be saved if some way could be found to count people automatically. During the next ten years he invented a system to use punched cards to hold data. Each card had a number of columns and rows, dividing it into dozens of little boxes. A piece of data collected about someone during the census could be represented by punching out certain of the holes. Then, all the cards could be put into a machine, and the machine could add up all the holes in each position.

Hollerith made these cards on the same machines used by the mint to make dollar bills. He used his invention to save immense amounts of time during the 1890 census, and went on to found a company which was the forerunner of IBM.

In the late 1920's, Vannevar Bush built the first useful analog calculator at the Massachusetts Institute of Technology. Like the machines of Pascal and Babbage, it was mechanical, but technological developments in the meantime had made possible a much more complex machine. The machine was constructed of many gears and rods, and filled a small room. It was used to do the large number of multiplications necessary to find the answer to certain kinds of mathematical problems. Some of its principles were later used in the first actual computer, the ENIAC.

Until the 1930's, calculating machines were thought of as being used only for number crunching, that is, for solving mathematical problems that required many arithmetic operations. The goal was to use a machine to solve these problems much faster with fewer errors than humans could. During the thirties, however, work on more complicated calculating machines gradually led various people to think about a machine that could do more than just calculate. Such a machine would be able to perform conditional operations, would be electrical instead of mechanical, would be programmable, would have some kind of memory – would be more than a calculator. It would be a computer.

One of the first machines that could be called a computer was the Mark I, built at IBM by Howard Aiken between 1939 and 1944. Like other early computers, it was built primarily for use in the war. Weapons had become sufficiently complex so that lengthy calculations were required to do things like aim long range artillery or set bombing sights. The military needed machines that could do these calculations faster than people.

The Mark I was the first large, digital computer. However, it was not electronic. It was electro-mechanical. That means that it used mechanical relays to open and close electronic circuits. The relays, in turn, were raised and lowered by electronic signals. But the relays themselves were still mechanical, and very slow compared to a completely electronic device.

Another electro-mechanical device was built at Iowa State University by John Atanasoff and Clifford Berry in 1942. Atanasoff invented several new ways of designing a computer. Although his machine was not widely used, many of his ideas were adopted in building the first true, electronic, digital computer, the ENIAC.

The ENIAC (Electronic Numerical Integrator And Calculator) was built by a team headed by J. Presper Eckert and John Mauchly, at the University of Pennsylvania, between 1943 and 1946. The ENIAC was built for the army and expected to perform the same kinds of military calculations as the Mark I. Unlike that machine, however, the ENIAC was completely electronic. Instead of using mechanical relays to switch circuits on and off, it used vacuum tubes, the same kind that were used in radios.

The ENIAC used over 18,000 vacuum tubes, which made it very large – about a hundred feet long, ten feet high, and three feet wide. It had a memory and was programmable and far faster than any calculating machine yet built. Everything that the ENIAC could do can be done today by a small desk-top computer.

While Mauchly and Eckert were working on ENIAC, their work came to the attention of John von Neumann, a mathematician who was working on the atomic bomb project. Von Neumann saw that the ENIAC would be useful for doing some of the long mathematical computations required by his work. As a result, he became a consultant to the ENIAC project and contributed some important ideas to it. He also helped write a number of reports in which the ideas being developed on the ENIAC project were systematically set forth, and expanded. The design of a computer, as described in these reports, is, with slight changes, the design of all modern computers, and it is often referred to as 'the von Neumann machine.'

One of the most important characteristics of the von Neumann machine is that it has a stored program.

All computers keep in their memory many instructions. Each instruction is represented in memory by a number (ones and zeros), and each instruction can make the computer do one limited operation, like move a number from memory to a register, or add a number in one register to that in another. All programs consist of these instructions, used over and over again in different combinations. What the combination of instructions is depends on what the program is supposed to do.

In the ENIAC, the user had to figure out ahead of time what instructions to use and in what order, and connect the appropriate memory locations to the CPU by hand, using cables that could be plugged into a patch panel, something like an old telephone switchboard. Once a program was patched in, the sequence of instructions could not be changed until the program was finished running.

After the ENIAC was built, a second computer, called EDVAC was built at the University of Pennsylvania. EDVAC (Electronic Discrete Variable Automatic Computer) was a stored program machine. Unlike earlier machines, a stored program machine keeps in its memory a program which is built out of instructions and resides in a complete form in memory. Each instruction in the program is labeled so that the CPU can run the program itself, by bringing each instruction in from memory.

This means that the CPU can not only run the program from beginning to end, but it can change its course in the middle, by selecting an instruction out of sequence. Thus a single program can be run in different sequences depending on external conditions. This results in a great deal of flexibility. All modern computers are stored program machines.

The first stored program computer to be completed was EDSAC, in 1949, at the University of Cambridge in England. EDVAC was completed in 1951, the same year as another stored program computer was built by Mauchly and Eckert for Sperry-Rand. This computer was the famous UNIVAC, the first commercial, electronic, digital computer. With UNIVAC's delivery to the Bureau of the Census, the era begun by Hollerith had come full circle, and a new age of computers was underway.

Throughout most of the nineteen-fifties, large vacuum tube computers were made by such companies as IBM, Remington-Rand (UNIVAC), and Burroughs. These machines were used for scientific calculations, and for a few commercial data-processing jobs. They were the first generation of modern computers.

All the computers discussed so far were vacuum tube machines. In 1948 at the Bell Laboratories, John Bardeen, Walter Brattain and William Shockley invented a transistor. In 1956 they received a Nobel Prize for this work. The transistor performs the same functions as a vacuum tube, but it is tiny in comparison and uses far less electricity. With the transistor, new possibilities in computers were opened up. In 1959 the first transistor-based, digital computers were delivered in significant numbers. The solid-state era had begun, and with it, the second generation of computers.

Transistors brought greater speed, smaller size and increased flexibility. By the beginning of the second generation, internal memories had advanced from crude, early forms like mercury delay lines and electrostatic charges to magnetic drum and magnetic core memories, and tape storage had made an appearance. Because transistors occupied a fraction of the space that vacuum tubes did, second generation computers could be much smaller. Also, computers with much more power could be built and take up no more space.

Second generation computers had more sophisticated memories. Magnetic core memories became very efficient, as did tape storage. In the mid-60s systems were built with disk storage devices. Computers were used more and more for commercial data processing in banks and other large institutions, as well as for military, government and scientific purposes. The leading companies during these years, roughly the sixties, included IBM, NCR, UNIVAC and Burroughs. Control Data Corporation was founded during this time.

In 1964 the third generation of computers made their first appearance. Generally, the third generation, which is still current, is identified with the use of integrated circuits, although some third generation computers used few integrated circuits.

An integrated circuit is a 'chip' of silicon on which thousands of microscopic transistors can be produced. Integrated circuits are made by depositing thin layers of metal and semiconductive material on the chip, which is about a quarter inch square. The semiconductive material is silicon to which one of several impurities has been added. Certain arrangements of this material and metal on the chip act like transistors, and are, in effect, microscopic transistors.

Parts of each layer on the chip are removed using microscope photographic techniques, leaving arrangements of these transistors and lines which carry current among them. The circuitry on such a 'chip' is more complicated than that of the entire ENIAC.

By the early seventies, integrated circuits could be mass produced cheaply enough to make possible inexpensive computers whose entire CPU was on a single chip called a microprocessor. At first the new microcomputers were built by hobbyists, but soon products like the Apple, the TRS-80, the Commodore PET and others proved that people could buy these small computers for their home and small businesses.

The result of all this is that today more and more people are learning about computers and using them. The computer power that only fifteen years ago was available only to large corporations and government agencies now costs half the price of an automobile, or less. Some computers cost as little as eighty dollars. In the field of computer technology, new discoveries are made virtually every day. Improvements come along so fast that it is impossible for one person to keep up with all of them. The search for ways to make tasks easier, that began when a person first counted on his fingers, has never stopped.

Many people believe that the computer will change the way we live. It certainly has and will change the way we communicate, exchange money, obtain entertainment, share information and manufacture goods. It also has and will deprive many people of their jobs and create new jobs for many other people. It will allow the government to keep track of people more easily and it will allow people to communicate with each other more easily. It will allow us to do many things more easily and quickly. However, it will not automatically make our lives more pleasant or meaningful. That is up to us.

PROGRAMMING LANGUAGES

A program, as we have seen, is a sequence of instructions which direct the computer through the performance of a job. Every program is written in a kind of code. That is because computers do not understand human languages. For example, if you want a computer to add two numbers together, you could sit down at the computer's keyboard and type "Add two plus two and print the answer." You could, but nothing much would happen. If, however, you coded your instruction in this form: PRINT 2 + 2 and then pressed return or enter, the computer might print the number 4. It would do this if it understood the language called BASIC. The word PRINT is a part of the BASIC code, as is the sign ' + ', meaning addition.

In other words, BASIC is a list of words that the computer understands. Using these words, you can make the computer do almost anything you want. Of course, dozens of computer languages exist besides BASIC. Each of these is a code that translates human commands into something the computer can understand. What the computer understands is something called its instruction set.

The Instruction Set

An instruction set is a number of commands which the CPU of a computer can understand and obey. Each command tells the CPU to do one very simple thing, such as move a number from a memory address to a register. Every kind of CPU has its own instruction set, at least slightly different from the instruction sets of other kinds of CPUs.

For example, most popular home computers use a microprocessor as their CPU; the Motorola 6800 and 68000 series, the Intel 8080, 8085 and 8088, the Zilog Z80 and Z8000 are all popular microprocessors. Each one of them has its own, unique instruction set. However, all these instruction sets have a lot in common. In fact, on the whole, the instructions in all these instruction sets do more or less the same things. But the code for each instruction is very different. One microprocessor cannot understand instructions from another microprocessor's instruction set.

The reason for this lies in the nature of an instruction. Let's look at a typical instruction for the Intel 8085 microprocessor, whose instruction set contains a little more than 80 instructions. One of these is the logic instruction Compare Register. This instruction compares a register that the programmer chooses with the accumulator (another, special register). What this means is that the CPU subtracts the number in the designated register from the number in the accumulator.

Then, depending on the result of this subtraction, certain flags are set. This means that certain bits in a special register are changed from one to zero or from zero to one. When a bit is used to record a condition in this way, it is called a flag. Later instructions can look at these flags to find out what the outcome of this instruction was.

Now that we know what the Compare Register instruction does, let's see what it looks like. It has two forms. One looks like this: CMP r, where r is replaced by a letter that stands for the register to compare with the accumulator. The other way of writing this instruction looks like this 10111xxx, where each x becomes either a one or zero depending on which register is being designated. The first way of writing this instruction is called assembly language. The second way is called machine language.

Now every microprocessor may have an instruction like Compare Register, but for each microprocessor its code will be different. The similar instruction for the Motorola 6502, for example, is 1100xxxx. Furthermore, the 6502 and the 8085 have different numbers of registers. So you see that one microprocessor's instruction set will not work on another microprocessor.

Earlier, we said that any CPU actually only does two kinds of things: moves numbers from one place to another, and performs arithmetic operations on numbers. Now you will see that instructions in the instruction set actually do these two kinds of things. But how does this translate into a complicated job like word processing or designing an airplane?

Remember the definition of digital. The whole idea behind digital computers is that anything can be described with numbers. We have seen that alphabet letters are represented by numerical codes, like the ASCII code.

When you use a word processor, you type in text, and each character goes to one memory location. The CPU can take any character from one memory location and put it in another under control of the instruction set. If it takes enough characters (represented by numbers) it can move whole paragraphs, change margins and do any of the other things a word processor does.

Similarly, any picture, for instance, that of an airplane part, is composed of thousands of tiny dots, and each dot may be represented by a number in a memory location. The value of the number may represent the dot's color, brightness, or other attributes. So a very complex picture can be represented in the computer's memory by a lot of numbers, and using the instruction set, a CPU can move these numbers around any which way. Once it can do that, it can be used in designing anything that can be drawn.

By now you should see that a computer can do very complicated jobs, even though it only does two kinds of things. You see, computers are actually very simple.

Machine Language

Let's look again at the machine language version of our Compare Register instruction: 10111xxx. If the xxx were replaced with, say, 000, the CPU would use the B register in its comparison. If the xxx were replaced with 100 the CPU would compare the H register. Thus the ones and zeros in an instruction are code for what the CPU is to do and for the location of the numbers it is to do it to. In our example, the first five digits, 10111, tell the CPU to compare a register's content to that of the accumulator. This part of the instruction is called the operator. The last three digits tell the CPU what to compare to the accumulator, and this part of the instruction is called the operand.

Assembly Language

As you might think, however, it is very difficult for a programmer to remember a lot of ones and zeros. That is why assembly language was invented. In assembly language, each instruction in the instruction set is represented not by ones and zeros, but by words of two or three letters, such as CMP for Compare. Now that is a lot easier to remember that ones and zeros, so it is called a mnemonic, from the Greek word for memory. A mnemonic is any word that sounds something like what it stands for, so that it is easier to remember.

A programmer using assembly language can write his program in mnemonics, and then a special program called an assembler will automatically convert his mnemonics into machine language, so that the microprocessor can understand it. As you may have surmised, every kind of microcomputer must use a different assembler.

High Level Languages

Even though assembly language is composed of mnemonics, it is still difficult to use. This is so partly because even mnemonics are a little hard to remember, but even more so because the instructions perform such tiny tasks. That means that a program must contain a very large number of instructions, and it is hard to keep track of so many of them.

One way to make this easier is to group the instructions into routines. For example, in a program you might want to display the message "Hit the return key" several times. Displaying this message requires a number of assembly instructions. Those instructions must move the code numbers for each letter in the message to the right places to get the message onto the screen.

However, once a programmer has written a group of instructions that displays the message, he may give it a label and stick it somewhere in memory. From then on, all he has to do is use one instruction (the CALL instruction) to put that group into action, and the message will be displayed. Such a group of instructions is called a routine.

High level languages are composed of words, as are assembly and machine languages. But whereas the binary words of machine language and the mnemonic words of assembly language stand for one instruction each, each word of a high level language stands for a whole routine. For example, the BASIC instruction ' + ' calls a routine. The various instructions in that routine find the numbers to be added, send them to one or more registers, add them together in a register and store the result in still another register.

Compilers And Interpreters

When writing a program in a high level language, a programmer uses the words of that language to compose what is called source code. Of course, before the computer can use the program, this source code must be changed into machine language, or object code: that is, ones and zeros. (We have already seen that even assembly language must be changed into machine language by an assembler.)

Two kinds of programs, called language processors, do this changing. One kind is a compiler and the other kind is an interpreter. A compiler changes the entire source code into machine language in one pass. The result is an object code program that is ready to run. An interpreter changes the source code into machine language while the program is running, one statement at a time, so no object code program ever exists as such.

Some Common High Level Languages

Over the years, many high level languages have been developed. Some of these are best suited to scientific uses, others to business uses, still others to educational uses. Some are suited only to very specialized uses, others can do many different kinds of jobs. Some are easy to learn, but take longer to run; some are very fast but hard to learn. Each has some advantages and some disadvantages, and new ones are being developed all the time.

As the above discussion implies, a high level language is really a program which recognizes certain words or statements, and can relate each word to a computer's instruction set. Such a program usually provides the programmer with information about mistakes he might make.

The language itself – the program – is recorded on some medium of mass storage, as is any other program, and can be transferred to memory and then run. Languages are also often stored permanently in ROM, so that as soon as the computer is turned on, the language is available.

The following six examples are representative of a range of high level languages. They are all widely used today.

BASIC (Beginner's All-purpose Symbolic Instruction Code)

BASIC is perhaps the most widely known high level language. It is easy to learn and easy to use. In fact, it was originally developed, in the mid-60s, as a learning aid, to teach beginners the fundamentals of programming. It was not intended to be used to write application programs; that is, programs used to perform actual, productive jobs. Nevertheless, it is now used for many applications in which speed is not vital.

BASIC is usually run as an interpreted language. For that and other reasons, it is relatively slow. On the other hand, it is easy to use. It has many built-in safeguards which identify mistakes that the programmer might have made. Its statements are almost all English words whose meanings are easy to remember.

Because it is so widely used, BASIC comes in many different versions, or dialects. All similar, each varies slightly from the rest. For example, the statement INPUT in one BASIC might be INKEY in another. Virtually all home computers run one or another version of BASIC, and most come with it either on disk or in ROM.

FORTRAN (FORmula TRANslation)

FORTRAN was one of the first high level languages. It was developed by people from IBM, along with some of their clients, in the last half of the 1950s. FORTRAN is a compiled language.

FORTRAN is very widely used, especially for scientific and engineering applications. It was designed with mathematical calculations in mind, although it is equally useful for other applications. FORTRAN is also used to teach programming.

FORTRAN has been used since its beginning on the largest computers, but it has also been adapted to small computers, including some home computers. However, as is true of many languages, FORTRAN for home computers cannot do as many things as it can on large computers.

The reason for this is memory size. A language program, as we saw above, must fit into internal memory and still leave room for the application program to be run. A language with many statements may not fit into a small computer. Therefore, shortened versions of the language have been developed for home computers.

COBOL (COmmon Business Oriented Language)

More application programs are written in COBOL than in any other language. It is most widely used in business, for all kinds of financial, management and record-keeping jobs. It was developed in the late 1950s by the United States government and a number of computer manufacturers and users.

COBOL statements are English words to a greater extent than most high level languages. All COBOL programs are divided into four parts: the identification division, the environment division, the data division and the procedure division.

The identification division simply identifies the program: its name, use, etc.

The environment division defines the devices which the program will use for input, output and mass storage.

The data division defines files. It tells what data will go into what file, and where in the file it will go.

The procedure division lists the data processing that will be done. In other words, it describes what the CPU is supposed to do to the data in the files.

PASCAL (Named for Blaise Pascal)

PASCAL was developed in the early 70s and was based on another language called ALGOL. PASCAL was designed to make it easier to write structured programs. Structured programming refers to a number of techniques for making it easier for people to read, change and correct errors in a program. One of the major structured features of

PASCAL is that its statements lend themselves to being organized in a pattern that parallels the actual flow of the program.

PASCAL also includes many error-checking features. These display messages if the programmer makes a mistake; for instance, if he uses a statement incorrectly, or spells it wrong, or leaves out one of a pair of statements that always go together. This speeds up programming, and results in finished programs that contain few errors.

PASCAL is used widely and is increasing in popularity.

LOGO (Named after the Greek word for 'word')

LOGO is a relatively simple language used primarily in education. It was developed to introduce young children to the fundamental principles of geometry and computer programming. It is very easy to learn.

The distinctive feature of LOGO is the use of figures called turtles which students can program. First, students may use actual mechanical turtles, that move around on the floor and can draw lines on large pieces of paper as they move. Then, students can program little pictures of turtles, which move about on a computer display. This procedure teaches children the relationship between physical shapes in space and their abstract counterparts in geometry. At the same time, of course, they absorb the basic concept of programming: that a machine can be made to perform tasks in response to a properly ordered sequence of simple instructions.

BASIC COMMANDS

As we mentioned above, most home computers use their own dialect of BASIC. It would take a book to explain all the instructions in one of those dialects, and several books to explain all the dialects of BASIC used by popular home computers. However, all BASICs have a lot in common.

The following discussion presents the most elementary BASIC instructions, which will be found in one form or another in all dialects of BASIC. We will discuss the function of each instruction, rather than its exact form, since that will differ from one dialect to another. The instructions are grouped into eight functional categories: arithmetic operators, display statements, memory allocation, control statements, data statements, input/output, and program statements.

Arithmetic and Logical Operators

These instructions are the most similar from dialect to dialect, and even in many other languages. They are used to perform arithmetic operations and to compare numbers logically.

Addition is usually symbolized by the plus sign: +. For example, the statement 2 + 3 would tell the CPU to add the numbers two and three and store the result in a special location reserved for arithmetic results.

Subtraction is usually symbolized by the minus sign: −. Similar to the plus sign, it tells the CPU to subtract the second of two numbers from the first. For example, the statement 3 − 2 would leave a one in the special location.

Multiplication is symbolized by the asterisk: ∗. The statement 3∗2 would tell the CPU to store a 6 in the special location.

Division is symbolized by the slash mark: /. This symbol means divide the first number by the second. 6/2 would store a 3 in the special location.

Now what if you wanted to perform more than one arithmetic operation at a time? For example, say you write 2∗3 + 6/4. The CPU would not know what you meant. You might mean multiply two and three, add six to the result, divide that result by four. Or you might mean add three to six, multiply that by two and divide by four. You might even mean multiply two by three and add to that the result of 6 divided by four.

BASIC has a built in rule that tells the CPU what you mean. The rule is, perform all multiplications and divisions first, then perform additions and subtractions. So the result you would get from the statement you wrote would be 7.5, because the CPU would first multiply two and three to get 6, then divide 6 by 4 to get one and a half, and then go back and add the two together.

So how can you get the result you wanted, which is three? By using parentheses to tell the CPU how you want the operations grouped. The parentheses are used as arithmetical operators. All operations inside parentheses are performed before those outside parentheses.

For example, if you wrote your statement like this: $(2*3+6)/4$, the CPU would first multiply two and three, then add six and finally divide the result by four. The answer would be three.

Logical operators are similar to arithmetic ones in that they affect numbers. We will discuss the three most often used ones.

Greater than (written $>$) is used to see whether or not one number is bigger than another. For instance, the statement, $5>2$ (five is greater than two) is true. The statement $4>4$ is false.

Less than (written $<$) is used to see whether or not one number is smaller than another. The statement $3<1,234$ is true.

Equal to (written $=$) is used to see whether or not one number is the same as another. The statement $4=4$ is true. The statement $4=4.4$ is false.

Display Statements

These statements tell the CPU to put something on the CRT display. Different dialects of BASIC use many variations of these instructions, but essentially, they all do one of two things: display text or display graphics (pictures).

The most common word for a text display instruction is PRINT. PRINT means display text. It may also mean send text to a printer or a file in mass storage, but we will stick to the display meaning. Fundamentally, a PRINT statement consists of the PRINT instruction and the thing to be displayed. This may be either a variable or a literal.

A variable is a label which stands for a memory location. If you PRINT a variable, the CPU displays the content of that location. For example, the statement PRINT A will display whatever number is stored at the memory location labeled A. (For how a memory location gets labeled, see assignment statements, below.)

A literal is a number or phrase that does not stand for something else. In most BASIC dialects, the statement PRINT "A" would result in the display of the letter A.

The other fundamental display statement is PLOT, or something like it. This instruction is accompanied by two numbers, the x and y coordinates of the point on the display where something is to be displayed. PLOT is a graphics command. It is used to display dots, not alphanumeric characters. These dots comprise a picture.

Most home computers are capable of more than one degree of precision in a graphics display. By precision we mean the number of dots that fit on a screen. The more dots, the finer detail the picture may have. Displays with relatively few dots (say 40 by 40) are called low resolution (lo-res), and displays with relatively many dots (say 500 by 500) are called high resolution (hi-res). Lo-res dots actually look more like small rectangles and are themselves composed of several hi-res dots.

An example of a PLOT statement might be PLOT 20,20. Assuming we had already told the CPU that we want to be in lo-res graphics, this statement would put a rectangle at the center of a 40 by 40 dot display.

Assignment Statements

In the last section we said that a variable is actually a memory location, and the value of that variable is the number stored in that memory location. Now we will see how the CPU assigns a variable to a specific location.

In a BASIC program, you might find the statement A = 3, or LET

A = 3. That means that the value of three is assigned to the variable A. The letter A is actually a label for the next open memory location in that part of the memory map used for storing variables. The statement A = 3 stores the number 3 at that memory location.

From then on, whenever the CPU encounters the letter A, standing alone, it will treat it as if it were the value in that memory location. If the CPU came to the statement PRINT A + 2 it would display the number 5. (We specify that a variable label must stand alone to be treated as such. If it were in quotes it would be treated as the letter A, itself. If it were a part of an instruction, like SAVE, it certainly would not be treated as a variable.)

Now, at another point, the program might contain the statement A = 6. That would change the value of the variable A. From then on, the CPU would treat the letter A, standing alone, as if it were the number 6. That is why it is called a variable. Its value may vary as a result of new assignment statements.

The LET = form of the assignment statement, or something like it, assigns both a value and a label to a memory location. The other major assignment statement in BASIC does not use a label. It uses the actual address of the memory location. This is the POKE instruction.

POKE puts a number directly into any location in internal memory. The location may be used as a variable or anything else. This makes POKE a very versatile instruction. It is also a very dangerous one, since if you put a number into the wrong memory address you could render an entire program unworkable.

The POKE instruction looks like this: POKE m,n. In this form, m stands for a memory address and n stands for the number to be put there. Thus, if you wanted to put the number 5 in the memory location 16305 you could use the instruction POKE 16305,5.

Memory Allocation

We have already touched on this subject in our discussion of variables in the preceding section, and in the earlier discussion of memory maps. Remember that each CPU uses different regions of internal memory to store different kinds of data, among them strings and variables. Both these kinds of data may be organized into arrays. You might think of an array as a honeycomb full of cells. The whole honeycomb is given a label, like A, for a variable array. Each cell has a sub-label. For example, the array may be one long honeycomb, a chain of cells, in which case it is a one-dimensional array. In a one-dimensional array each cell is given a label like A(1), A(2), A(3) and so on.

The array may also be two dimensional, with a width and length, in other words, the honeycomb is so many cells wide and so many cells long. Each cell would be labeled like this: A(1,1), A(1,2) . . . A(3,1), A(3,2) . . . etc.

Arrays may even have three or more dimensions. What we are interested in here, however, is not arrays, but memory allocation. The CPU must know how many locations to set aside in the appropriate memory region for each array. To tell it, we use the DIM instruction.

DIM is a mnemonic for the word dimension. If we knew that in our program we were going to use a two-dimensional variable array labeled A which would have four cells in one dimension and 5 cells in the other dimension, we would use a DIM instruction somewhere in the program before the first use of the array. The full DIM statement would look like this: DIM A(4,5)-or something similar, depending on the BASIC dialect. This statement tells the CPU to set aside a total of 20 memory locations for that array, and to label them as A(1,1) through A(4,5).

Control Statements

As we have seen, a program is a list of instructions which the CPU obeys in some sequence. We also saw that one of the important characteristics of all modern computers is that they can be programmed to change that sequence depending on some condition.

For example, a program might count the number of people who go in and out of an elevator. One set of instructions would deduct one from the total whenever a person exited. Another set of instructions would add a number to the total whenever someone entered. A third set of instructions would decide whether someone has just exited or entered. Depending on which of these two conditions is true (someone has entered or someone has exited), the CPU would either follow one or the other set of instructions that add or deduct from the total. This is what we mean when we say that the computer can change the sequence of its own instructions.

A number of BASIC commands do this kind of thing. They are called control instructions because they decide which part of a program is going to control the next actions of the CPU. Let's look at a few of them.

GOTO: Remember that in BASIC each statement is given a line number, that is, a label for that statement. For example, we can tell the CPU to execute a program starting at line number 10 or line number

100 or wherever in the program we want. We do this with the GOTO command. A GOTO statement is the GOTO command followed by the next line number to be executed. For example, the statement GOTO 34 would cause the CPU to execute line number thirty-four next, and continue in order from there.

IF...THEN: This statement consists of two instructions and a condition in between. For example, in our elevator passenger counter, let's say that the routine that decides whether a passenger is exiting or entering sets a flag one way or the other. Let's say that that flag is the variable A. If a person is entering, A will be set to 1, if not it will be set to 0. Then we might use a statement like IF A = 1 THEN GOTO 100. (Assuming that line 100 was the first line of the routine that adds to the total.) If A were not equal to 1, the CPU would ignore everything after the word THEN.

FOR...NEXT: This is actually two statements. It is used to repeat an action over and over. For example, say you had a one-dimensional array with five cells, called A, and you wanted to fill every cell in it with the number 6. You could use a statement like: FOR I = 1 to 5 : A(I) = 6: NEXT I.

This line contains three statements, separated by colons. The first statement says that a variable I will equal each of the numbers from one through five, in turn; and for each of those turns you want to do something. The second statement says that what you want to do is make the cell labeled A(I) equal to 6; that is, A(1) when I equals 1, A(2) when I equals 2, and so on. The third statement simply tells the CPU to make I equal to the next value in this sequence.

GOSUB...RETURN: Here we have two instructions which always go together. GOSUB is like GOTO. It tells the CPU to jump to a certain line number, for example, GOSUB 100. But it also tells the CPU that as soon after line 100 as it meets a RETURN statement, to come back to where it started. For example, say the program looked like this:

```
  1    LET A = 2
 10    GOSUB 100
 20    LET A = 3
 30    GOSUB 100
 40    LET A = 4
 50    GOSUB 100
 60    END
100    PRINT A * 2
110    RETURN
```

Line number one assigns a value to the variable A. Line 10 tells the CPU to jump to line 100. There it would print 4 and then, on line 110, return and execute line 20. Again it would jump to line 100 and this time print 6, return, change the value of A a third time, jump to 100, print 8, return and, finally, end.

The two lines, 100 and 110 are called a subroutine, which is where the SUB in GOSUB comes from. You can see that this transfer of control saves the programmer from writing the subroutine three times. He simply writes it once and then uses a GOSUB. . .RETURN control structure whenever he wants to use the subroutine.

Data Statements

The data used by a typical home computer program normally comes from one of three sources. Someone enters it from the keyboard, it is already in internal memory or it comes from mass storage; that is, a diskette.

BASIC has a number of different instructions to use data from each of these sources, and these instructions differ among different BASIC dialects. In general, data from the first source, the keyboard, is handled by instructions like GET, INPUT, INKEY or similar instructions.

Each of these instructions has two forms, one which is used to handle numbers and another used for strings. For example, INPUT might be used with a number, and INPUT$ with a string. These instructions tell the CPU to stop and wait until something is typed, and to assign a variable to whatever is typed next. Consider the statement, INPUT$ A$. That means that whatever is typed next, up to the first carriage return, will be treated as a string, and the symbol A$ will stand for that string.

Say you then typed 'Now is the time for all good men' and pressed the carriage return key. From then on, whenever the CPU saw the variable A$ it would treat it as that string. Later in the program, the statement PRINT A$ would cause the string, 'Now is the time for all good men' to be displayed on the CRT.

As we saw earlier, a variable is simply a memory location given a label. In our example, the symbol A$ is the label of some memory address where the string 'Now is the time for all good men' begins. (Of course a string of more than one letter takes up more than one address – one address for every letter to be exact.)

Remember the instruction POKE which put a number directly into a memory location? It has a companion, PEEK. The PEEK instruction lets you look directly at a memory location. Let's say you knew that the first character in the string A$ was located at memory address 20894. If you gave the CPU the instruction PRINT PEEK 20894 it would display the number 78 on the CRT. Seventy-eight is the ASCII code for the letter N. If you gave the instruction X$ = PEEK 20894 the CPU would create a new string variable, X$, which would consist of the single letter, N.

Another way to put data into internal memory and then use it is to carry the data in with the program. Most BASICs do this with some version of the READ...DATA instructions. The DATA statement consists of the DATA instruction followed by several data, separated by commas. It might look something like this: DATA 12,2,456,32.

The READ statement consists of the READ instruction and a variable, for example, READ A. Whenever the CPU saw the READ statement it would assign the next datum in the DATA statement to the variable A. Thus the first time the CPU saw READ A, it would make A = 12. The next time it would make A = 2, and so on.

So far we have seen some ways that BASIC handles data from the keyboard and from internal memory. Now let's see how it handles data from a diskette.

As we have seen, when the CPU sends data to a disk we say it writes to disk, and when it receives data from the disk we say it reads the disk. Data on a disk is kept in files, and each file is given a name. By using the name, the CPU can read data from or write it to a specific file. In fact, it can even read and write data to a specific part of a file. Again, different BASIC dialects use different forms of the same instructions to access data on a disk. A common form for these instructions is: OPEN, READ, WRITE, CLOSE.

The OPEN command is followed by a file name, and tells the disk drive controller to send data to or from that file on the disk.

The READ and WRITE commands do just that, either bring data from or send it to a disk, and to the OPENed file.

The CLOSE command simply closes the file, so that the entire system knows that the read or write operation has been concluded.

File Handling

All BASICs designed to be used with disks include some form of the instructions for initializing disks and transferring entire files between memory and disk. You may wonder what the difference is between transferring files between disk and memory and reading/writing the data in a file to and from memory. The difference is that we are talking about different kinds of files.

The files that are read/written are text files, or data files. They contain data to be used by a program: files of text or a word processing program, files of figures for an accounting program, files of addresses for a mailing list program. Remember that programs are kept in files too, and this is the kind of file which is transferred as a whole into memory, so that the program it contains may then be run.

The BASIC instructions used to handle program files are INIT, SAVE, LOAD and DELETE, or something similar, depending on the dialect. INIT is a mnemonic for initialize. It causes the disk to be initialized, a process we discussed earlier in the section on mass storage. No disk is usable until it has been initialized on the computer with which it will be used.

SAVE and LOAD are used to actually transfer program files to and from memory. SAVE takes the program in memory and puts it on a disk in the form of a file. Usually when the SAVE instruction is given it is accompanied by a file name. For example, SAVE Checking would transfer the program in memory onto a disk and name the file Checking, which would be a good name for a program used to balance your checkbook.

The LOAD command is the opposite of SAVE. It transfers the file from the disk into memory. The file stays on the disk, by the way. For example, the instruction LOAD Checking would transfer a copy of the program in the file called Checking into the memory. If you then changed the program you might want to SAVE it under a different name, say Checking2. You would then have two files on the disk, one containing the original program and another containing a new version of the program.

DELETE, as you may have guessed, gets rid of the file altogether. For example, having put the file Checking2 on your disk, you might decide you no longer need the file Checking. You could then give the instruction DELETE Checking, and that file would be erased from the disk.

Program Statements

Finally, we will discuss a few typical BASIC instructions used to operate programs. These are LIST, NEW, RUN and REM.

The LIST instruction simply tells the CPU to display the program source code on the CRT. Of course, most programs are too long to fit on the screen. Most computers will display one screen full of source code at a time, and continue after you press a key, such as the space bar.

The NEW instruction erases whatever program is in internal

memory. If you have just LOADed a program, and you decide you want to get rid of it without LOADing a different one, you simply type NEW. You might do this if you want to start writing your own program from scratch.

RUN is the instruction which tells the CPU to start executing the program. If the program is already in memory you simply type RUN. If not, some BASIC dialects let you type RUN followed by the file name, thus loading and running the program in a single step.

The single most important instruction for many programs does not tell the CPU to do anything. This is the REM instruction, or something like it in various dialects. The REM instruction is used within a program to tell the CPU to ignore whatever follows it on a line of program code.

This lets the programmer put in notes in English, explaining the code, to help him remember what it means later and to let other people understand it. This is called documenting a program. The best program in the world is virtually useless if it is not documented, which is why the REM statement is so important.

STRUCTURED PROGRAMMING

The three desirable characteristics of any computer program are clarity, economy and efficiency. Clarity means anyone should be able to look at the source code and see how the program works – what each part does and how the parts interact. Economy means that the program uses the least amount of a computer's resources to get the job done. These resources are processor time and memory space. Efficiency means that the source code itself is concise.

All programs consist of two fundamental parts: algorithms and data structures.

An algorithm is a procedure which, when followed, produces a solution to a problem. In terms of a program, an algorithm is a sequence of instructions which solves a single problem. The problem may be to display instructions on a CRT, to take input from the keyboard or to perform some complicated mathematical computation.

An example of a very simple problem would be to keep track of how many people were on an elevator. As we saw in an earlier discussion, the algorithm for doing this might consist of three parts, one to decide if a person were entering or exiting the elevator, another to add to the count if a person were entering, and a third to subtract from the count if a person were exiting.

As you may have noticed, each of these parts also requires an algorithm. For instance, the algorithm for adding to the count would be to identify the variable that represents the count and add one to it. (Or increment it, as a programmer would say.) This is a very simple, or trivial, algorithm. A programmer would write the code for this algorithm without even thinking about it.

Now, algorithms must have something to manipulate, and of course, what they manipulate is data. In our example, the data is the count of people in the elevator. The structure for this data would be a variable. As the count changed, the value of this variable would change. A data structure, then, is a method for organizing data.

A variable is a trivially simple kind of data structure. When computer scientists discuss data structures they usually are referring to large data bases in which much information must be stored. How to store a lot of information depends on what kind of information it is and how it will be manipulated. A data base of numbers to be manipulated in plotting the course of a moon shot would be structured differently than a data base full of account records used by a bank, and that would be structured differently than the information in a mail order company's catalog mailing list.

How to structure data in the best way for a given purpose has been one of the central concerns of computer science since it began. A number of ways exist, some of which we have already touched on, such as files and arrays. Others include look-up tables, queues, stacks, lists and trees.

The problem facing every programmer is to choose algorithms and data structures that will maximize the clarity, economy and efficiency of his program. Now there is a right way to compose a program and a wrong way. But it is not always easy to tell what the right way is. How can a programmer tell what the best algorithms and data structures will be for a new program? Over the years, since computer programming began in the early 1940s, computer scientists have developed a number of techniques to help the programmer solve this problem.

Some of these techniques are sophisticated mathematical analyses, by which the value of a given algorithm or data structure may be predicted. Others have to do with using a methodical, systematic approach in designing any program. The latter, as a group, are called structured programming.

Structured programming is simply a collection of methods for designing clear, efficient, economical programs. Put simply, structured programming means logical organization.

For example, all programs can be broken down into parts, as we saw with our elevator example. These parts are sometimes called modules. Each module performs a task. Also, each module may consist in turn of smaller modules. In fact, the entire program may be thought of, at its highest level, as a giant module.

Within this module are smaller modules, at the next lower level, each of which performs a major function within the program, say input of data. Within each of these, at the next lower level, are smaller modules which perform smaller tasks, say inputting data from the keyboard. At the very lowest level, each module would perform very small tasks indeed, such as reading a single keystroke.

This picture of a program as a sort of pyramid, or as nested modules, is the foundation of structured programming. Conceived of this way it is easier to keep track of each part of a program and to remember how it interacts with other parts. A program written in this form is easier to understand and to document. It is also easier to write in the first place and will contain few errors. Finally, if it does contain some errors, as most programs do, those errors will be easier to locate and correct.

Program Design

When designing a program, the programmer starts with as complete as possible a description of what the program is to do. The more detail in this description, the better.

The next step is to start writing down the modules, in the pyramid form described above. This becomes a kind of branching structure in which each module is represented by a box and labeled with a brief description. Each box is connected by a line drawn from the higher level module of which it is a part. All modules that are at the same level in terms of the program are drawn at the same level on this system chart.

Now the system chart emphasizes the relationship among the modules, the shape of a program. It does not show details of how a program works, that is, the flow of control. For that, a flowchart is used, as we will see in a moment.

Using a system chart is consistent with an approach to programming called top-down design. This means that you start with the highest level and decide what major modules a program will have. Then you break each of these into smaller modules, and so on until in the last step you actually write the algorithms that constitute the program code.

In practice, however, it seldom works out so neatly. Sometimes you have to write an algorithm first and adapt the organization of modules to the way that algorithm works. For example, the best algorithm for a certain task may require that data be sent to it in a certain form. That in turn may require changing the relationship among some higher level modules which handle data.

In the end, most programs are designed from both ends toward the middle. Top down design helps a programmer visualize the overall structure of a program before he starts filling in the working parts. Bottom up design ensures that the working parts really work, before building a structure around them.

Another aspect of the system chart is that each module has only one entry and one exit. This has important implications. As long as a module is connected to only one module above it and one below it, it can be changed relatively easily. One module may be taken out of the system and a new one plugged in, and the new one would only have to accept data from the higher module and produce it for the lower one in the same form as its predecessor. Whatever processing goes on inside the module would be independent of its neighbors.

However, if a module is connected to a lot of different other modules things get complicated. It may take data in different forms from different modules. Part of the internal working of the module would then be devoted to determining which kind of data it is processing. Replacing such a module becomes extremely difficult, since in this kind of a program, every module is affected by the internal processing of other modules. Replacing such a module invariably has ramifications that are impossible to foresee.

It should be apparent now why it is easier to work with a program in which every module has only one input and one output. This idea is at the heart of the concept of structured programming.

A flowchart, like a system chart, consists of boxes. In both kinds of charts the shapes of these boxes represent the kind of activity taking place in that module. Each kind of activity is shown by a different shape.

The kinds of boxes used in flow charts are divided into three categories: basic, specialized and additional. Many programmers do not use flowcharts, or only use sketchy ones. They only use a few of the many kinds of boxes, enough to give a general idea of the flow of a program without spending too much time on a flowchart. The commonly used boxes, or symbols, are the oval, the rectangle, the diamond, the parallelogram, and the arrow.

The oval is a terminal, that is the beginning or end of the program. A rectangle stands for processing of some kind. A diamond is a point at which the program makes a decision. A parallelogram is input or output. All these boxes are connected by arrows, which show the direction in which control is flowing.

To illustrate, let's flowchart our elevator passenger counting program. We start with an oval, to indicate the beginning.

BEGIN

Assuming we start with an empty elevator, the first thing the program will do is designate a data structure, in this case a variable, and initialize it to zero. In BASIC this might be done with a statement like LET $C = 0$, where C stands for count. (We could also write $COUNT = 0$, but that takes up more memory space.) In our flowchart this step would look like this:

INIT
COUNT

As we run our program, the next thing to happen would be input from some sensing device, in the form of one of two signals, one for an entering passenger, one for an exiting passenger. We might call this, simply, change.

INPUT
CHANGE

Our program's next action would be to decide whether the change is an entry or exit. This would involve some way of reading and discriminating between the two kinds of signals, but for our sketchy flowchart we will just write:

ENTRY?

This last part of the diagram alters the flow by making a decision. If the answer to the question is yes, we want to increment that count.

INCREMENT
COUNT

Otherwise, we want to decrement it (subtract one).

DECREMENT
COUNT

Obviously, we want to keep running the program indefinitely. We do not want to count only one change in the number of passengers. Therefore, this program will be in the form of a continuous loop. Having either incremented or decremented the count, we then go back to the point at which we are ready to sense another change. This is shown by an arrow, and the whole flowchart looks like this:

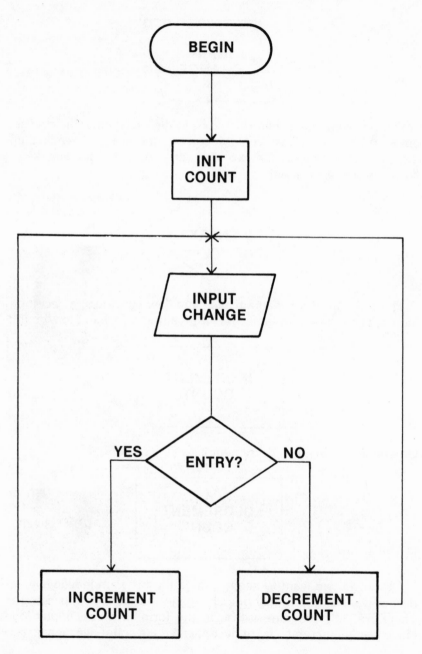

KEYBOARDS AND SPECIAL KEYS

In this section we will look at the keyboards, and discuss the special keys of six popular home computers, Apple II, ATARI 800, TRS-80 Model III, IBM-PC, Texas Instruments 99/4A and Commodore VIC-20.

One key which we can mention right off the bat is the one that prints a character that looks like this: ^ . Called a caret, this character signifies the mathematical operation of exponentiation; that is, raising a number to some power. As such it is not really a special key, but rather a character that is found on most computers, though not on typewriters.

APPLE II

The Apple II keyboard has 52 keys. Forty-four of these are the same as on a standard electric typewriter including two shift keys and a space bar. In addition, there are eight special keys, as follows:

CTRL The control key is used in conjunction with one or more other keys. The control key is pressed and held while a second and sometimes a third key is also pressed. This sends one of a variety of special codes to the CPU. What these codes do depends on what program is running at the time, but each control code also has a standard meaning taken from an earlier technology, teletype communications.

For example, the standard meaning of control-G is to cause the Apple's tiny loudspeaker to emit a single blip. This blip is hard to hear, but is still analogous to the old teletype signal bell, which is why the G key is labeled with the word 'bell'.

ESC The escape key, like the control key, is often used in conjunction with another key, but it may also be used alone. As with the control key, all that happens when you press the escape key is that a code is sent to the CPU. What the CPU does as a result depends on what program is running at the time. However, a common use for the escape key, and the reason for its name, is to provide a way to cancel the current program function.

For instance, a program may present the user with a series of menus. A main menu may allow the user to choose one of several sub-menus, and each sub-menu may allow the user to begin execution of some process. If, say, you made a wrong choice from a sub-menu and wanted to return to the sub-menu without completing the process you had choosen, you might use the escape key. Or you might use it to return to the main menu from a sub-menu without choosing any process. We would call this escaping to the main menu.

The escape key is also used with the A,B,C, and D keys to move the cursor right, left, down and up respectively while editing a program in BASIC. Escape is also used with E and F in BASIC program editing to erase lines or parts of lines.

RESET The reset key tells the CPU to stop everything it is doing and return to its original state. What actually happens is that a number of soft switches are reset. Soft switches are simply memory locations which hold some value used as a flag. For example, a certain memory location holds one of two numbers depending on whether the display is currently in graphics or text mode. On reset, the number for text is always sent to this location, causing the display to be in text.

Reset also causes the Apple II to cease running any program being executed and return control to whatever language was being used. In other words, reset can be used to stop a program, and after resetting the program may be run again. However, some programs set a soft switch that causes the reset to reboot whatever disk might be in the drive.

On some Apple IIs, the reset key does not function by itself, but only when the control key is pressed. This is a safeguard against hitting the reset key by mistake, which in some cases might lead to a loss of data.

REPT The repeat key is used to repeat automatically whatever key is being pressed, or in some programs, has last been pressed. If you hold down a key, and also hold down the repeat key, the effect is the same as if you repeatedly pressed the first key ten times a second.

← → The two arrow keys on the Apple II function as backspace keys on a typewriter, except that the one that points to the right moves the cursor forward instead of backward. In normal use, the arrow keys are what is called non-destructive. That means that if you use one to move the cursor over some text, the text is not erased. Only the position of the cursor is changed. This may be changed, however, by a given program.

SHIFT The Apple shift keys are like those of a typewriter except that they do not cause letters to be displayed in upper case. Normally, the Apple has no lower case, and the shift keys only affect the number keys and certain punctuation mark keys.

RETURN The return key is used as a carriage return and to send information to the CPU. As a carriage return key, it moves the cursor to the beginning of the next lower line. Also, anything typed at the keyboard must be followed by a return key before the CPU will become aware of it.

ATARI 800

The ATARI 800 keyboard has 61 keys. Unlike the Apple II, ATARI keys have auto-repeat. That means that if any key is held down for more than about one second, it will repeat itself until released. Forty-three of these keys are the same as on a standard electric typewriter, including two shift keys and a space bar. In addition, there are 18 special keys, as follows:

ESC The escape key is used primarily to allow the printing of fifteen graphics characters directly to the screen. These graphics characters are arrows and other symbols useful in programs. Each is printed by a different combination of keys which are pressed while the escape key is held down.

CLR-SET-TAB This key is used to set tabs, as on an electric typewriter, and to move the cursor to a tab position that has been set. It is used with the shift key to set a tap stop, with the control key to clear a tab stop, and by itself to move the cursor to a tab stop.

CTRL The control key is used in conjunction with the other keys. Each combination of the control key and one other alphabet key produces a special graphic shape which can be used to compose pictures on the display.

CLEAR Used with either the shift or control key, the clear key erases the display and moves the cursor to the upper left corner of the screen (the 'home' position).

INSERT Used with the shift key, the insert key moves all lines of text below the cursor down one line, creating space for a new line. Used with the control key it moves characters to the right of the cursor one space to the right, making space for a new character.

DELETE-BACK S This is the delete-back space key. It erases the character under the cursor and moves the cursor one space to the left, leaving a space. It is, therefore, what is called a destructive back space. Used with the shift key it erases the line on which the cursor is and moves lower lines up to take the removed line's place. Used with the control key it erases the character under the cursor and moves characters to the right one space to the left, to fill the hole.

BREAK The break key is a kind of reset which stops whatever program the computer is running. Its exact effect varies depending on the program.

ARROW KEYS The ATARI 800 has four arrow keys, one for each compass direction. Used with the control key these move the cursor non-destructively. Used without the control key these keys act as normal typewriter keys, each printing a different shifted and unshifted character.

CAPS-LOWR This key is like a typewriter shift-lock in reverse.

When it is depressed, all alphabet keys are displayed in lower case (unless the shift or control key is pressed with them for upper case or graphic character, respectively). Unlike a typewriter, the caps-lowr key only affects alphabet keys, not numbers or some punctuation marks.

(ATARI) One key is labeled with the ATARI corporate logo. This key causes characters to be displayed in inverse video. Inverse video means that instead of light on a dark background, the display will be dark on a light background. If the display is already inverse, pressing the key again will return the display to normal video.

RETURN The return key is used as a carriage return and to send information to the CPU. As a carriage return key, it moves the cursor to the beginning of the next lower line. Also, anything typed at the keyboard must be followed by a return key before the CPU will become aware of it.

The following four keys are located at the right of the other keys and are used to control cartridges. Cartridges are mass storage devices, comparable to tape cassettes, which store programs for games and other applications.

SYSTEM RESET Rewinds the installed cartridge to its beginning. If a program is running when system reset is pressed, it will be stopped.

SELECT Displays the first screen for the next program on the tape. Typically this display will be a menu from which you may choose various options.

OPTION Used to choose among the options on a menu or other display.

START Runs the next program on a cartridge or begins the option you have chosen.

TRS-80, MODEL III

The TRS-80, Model III keyboard has the usual typewriter keys, and twenty special keys. All keys have auto-repeat. That means that if any key is held down for more than about one second, it will repeat itself until released. The special keys are explained below.

NUMERIC KEYPAD This is a group of twelve keys to the right of the regular keyboard. The numeric keypad is used to work with numbers and is used as is a calculator. It consists of keys for each of the numbers 0 through 9, and a decimal point. The twelfth key is an enter key. An enter key is like a return key on the Apple or ATARI. When a number has been keyed in with the other numeric keys, the enter key must be pressed to send that number to the CPU.

BREAK This is a kind of reset key. It interrupts whatever the CPU is doing, including most programs being run.

SHIFT The shift key is used, among other things, to change from upper to lower case, but not the way that it does on a typewriter. Instead it is used in conjunction with the Ø key. Every time the shift key is pressed in conjuction with Ø, the Model III changes from upper to lower case, or from lower to upper case, depending on which one was in effect. Another use of shift, with the @ key, pauses any program being executed. Finally, shift with the down arrow and asterisk is used to make a printer print out whatever is on the screen.

← The left arrow key is a destructive backspace. Used with the shift key it returns the cursor to the beginning of the line.

→ The right arrow key tabs the cursor eight characters to the right. Used with the shift key, it converts the display to a 32 character line.

ENTER Enter is the same as the return on an Apple or ATARI. It is a carriage return, positioning the cursor on the far left of the next lower line, and it is also used to enter data that has been typed in.

UP AND DOWN ARROWS Move the cursor up and down a line at a time.

CLEAR This key erases the display and positions the cursor at the upper left corner of the screen (the 'home' position). It also changes the display to 64 characters per line if it was not already. Any key presses not already entered when clear is pressed are lost.

IBM-PC

The IBM-PC has the most keys of the popular home computers: 83 in all. In addition to the regular typewriter keys it has 25 special keys. All of them have auto-repeat.

FUNCTION KEYS On the far left of the keyboard are ten function keys, labeled F1 through F10. In BASIC, each has a special function, letting you type in a command with one keypress. These include LIST, RUN, LOAD and so on. One of them, F9, lets you change the function of any of the other keys, so what a function key does may depend on what you have programmed it to do.

A function key may perform different functions for different programs. When not in BASIC, but in the operating system, some of these keys have other special functions which control the display of lines of text.

NUMERIC KEYPAD On the right hand part of the keyboard are several keys which are used to work with numbers, like a calculator. Ten of these keys are for the numbers 0 through 9. Others are a decimal point key, an add key and a subtract key.

NUM LOCK When the number lock key is pressed, the numeric keypad is activated or de-activated, depending on which state it was already in.

HOME This is the same key as the numeric keypad 7. When the numeric keypad is de-activated, this key moves the cursor to the upper left corner of the screen (the 'home' position).

UP ARROW This is the same key as the numeric keypad 8. When the numeric keypad is de-activated, this key moves the cursor one line up.

← This is the same key as the numeric keypad 4. When the numeric keypad is de-activated, this key moves the cursor one space to the left, non-destructively.

→ This is the same key as the numeric keypad 6. When the numeric keypad is de-activated, this key moves the cursor one space to the right, non-destructively.

DOWN ARROW This is the same key as the numeric keypad 2. When the numeric keypad is de-activated, this key moves the cursor one line down.

END This is the same key as the numeric keypad 1. When the numeric keypad is de-activated, this key moves the cursor to the end of whatever line it is on.

INS This is the same key as the numeric keypad 0. When the numeric keypad is de-activated, this key puts the computer in insert mode. While in insert mode, a typed character will be inserted at the cursor position, and other characters moved to the right to make room for it. Pressing the insert key again will cancel insert mode.

DEL The delete key erases the character at the cursor position and pulls characters to the right of it back to fill the space.

← This left arrow key, near the upper right corner of the keyboard, is a destructive backspace. It moves the cursor to the left, erasing any characters over which it moves, leaving spaces where they were.

ESC The escape key has a specialized function and is used to change lines of program source code.

TAB ARROWS A key near the upper left corner of the keyboard is labeled with two arrows and is used to move the cursor to tab stops which are preset every eight spaces. Shifted, this key tabs to the left, unshifted, to the right.

CTRL The control key is used in conjunction with some other key to signal a command or function. What these are varies depending on the program or operating mode. An important use of control is with the key labeled SCR LOCK/BREAK. Pressing the control key with this key stops any program in progress.

SHIFT The shift key on the IBM-PC is marked by a wide arrow pointing upward. It is exactly like the shift on a typewriter and changes all lower case letters to capitals.

ALT Like the control key, the alternate key is used in conjunction with other keys to send various special signals to the CPU. An important combination of keys is CTRL + ALT + DEL, which is the IBM-PC reset signal, causing any disk in the system to reboot.

ENTER This key is labeled with an arrow shaped like a backward L. It is located between the alphabetic keys and the numeric keypad. It is a return key, used both to move the cursor to the beginning of the next lower line and to enter any data that has been typed.

CAPS LOCK This key changes the case in which keys are displayed. If the system is already in lower case, pressing caps lock will change all subsequently typed keys to upper case, and vice versa.

PRT SC Print screen, when pressed with the shift key, will cause a printer to print out whatever is on the screen.

COMMODORE VIC 20

The Commodore VIC 20 keyboard has sixty-nine keys. Some of these are special keys, and some are ordinary typewriter keys. The ordinary typewriter keys print both upper and lower case letters, numbers, and several other characters not usually found on a typewriter, such as upward and leftward pointing arrows, the English pound sign, the Greek letter pi. Most keys also print a third, graphic character- some shapes such as a line, a diamond, a rectangle or some other shape, all of which might be used as elements in a picture. These graphic characters are shown on the front side of their keys.

The VIC 20 also has several special keys.

(COMMODORE) This is the key at the lower left corner of the keyboard that bears the Commodore corporate logo. It is used, with the shift key, to switch between upper and lower case display. The Commodore key is also used in conjunction with the shift key and the ordinary typewriter keys to display the graphic characters.

SHIFT The shift keys are used as on an ordinary typewriter. When you have used the shift and Commodore keys to display in lower case, you use the shift key to type individual letters in upper case. Shift is also used in conjunction with various other keys that have both shifted and unshifted functions.

SHIFT LOCK This key does the same thing as the Commodore, shift combination, switches between upper and lower case.

CTRL The control key of the VIC 20, like that of other computers, has no effect by itself. It is used in conjunction with other keys to send various messages to the CPU. In this it is something like a shift key.

CURSOR UP-DOWN This key is near the bottom right of the keyboard. Unshifted, it moves the cursor down one line, non-destructively. Shifted, it moves it up one line, non-destructively.

CURSOR LEFT-RIGHT This key is to the right of the cursor up-down key. Unshifted, it moves the cursor one space to the right, non-destructively. Shifted, it moves the cursor one space to the left, non-destructively.

INST-DEL The insert delete key is in the upper right corner of the keyboard. Unshifted, it moves the cursor one space to the left, deletes the character there and pulls all characters to the right back to fill the resulting space; that is, it is a destructive backspace. Shifted, it opens a space to the left of the cursor where a new character may be inserted.

RVS ON-OFF The reverse on and reverse off keys share a key with the numbers 9 and 0, respectively. They can only be used in conjunction with the control key. Reverse on switches the display to inverse video: dark characters on a light background. Reverse off switches back to normal video, light characters on a dark background.

RUN-STOP The run-stop key is located on the left hand edge of the keyboard. Unshifted, it stops whatever program is in progress. If no program is running, it does nothing. Shifted, it loads a program from the cassette player.

RESTORE This key is used to stop a program that is waiting for input from the keyboard. It must be used with the Run-Stop key.

COLOR KEYS The keys for the numbers 1 through 8 are also color keys. Each bears the name of a color on its front side, and when used with the control key, changes the display to that color.

FUNCTION KEYS These eight keys are programmable. That means that part of a program may define what effect any of these keys will have. Any of these keys may thereby have the same effect as any combination of keys, thus saving keystrokes.

RETURN The return key on the VIC 20 has the same uses as on the other computers we have discussed.

TEXAS INSTRUMENTS 99/4A

The TI 99/4A has 48 keys. Many of them have not only a shifted and unshifted form, but a third form which is used in conjunction with a function key. The shifted and unshifted characters on a key are labeled on the top of the key, as with most keyboards. The function is labeled on the front side of the key. The space bar and all character keys have auto-repeat.

ALPHA LOCK This key is like a shift-lock on a regular typewriter, except that it is not held down when pressed. Rather each time you press it, it shifts case from upper to lower, or from lower to upper, depending on which was already in effect.

ENTER The enter key has the same uses as the return keys of other computers.

CTRL The TI control key is located near the bottom left of the keyboard. It is used only in conjunction with other keys to perform various functions, most of which are concerned with telecommunications.

FCTN The function key, as mentioned above, is used only in conjuction with other keys. The functions achieved in this way include cursor movement, line erase, character deletion, character insertion and others.